THE
CROSS
AND THE
CROWN

THE
CROSS
AND THE
CROWN

KESWICK MINISTRY

Edited by David Porter

OM Publishing
PO Box 300, Carlisle, Cumbria, UK CA3 0QS

Keswick Convention Council, England

Cover design: Mainstream

British Library Cataloguing in Publication Data

The Cross and the Crown: Keswick Ministry.
1. Bible—Critical studies
I. Porter, David *1945*–
220.6

ISBN 1-85078-117-6

OM Publishing is an imprint of Send The Light
(Operation Mobilisation),
PO Box 300, Carlisle, Cumbria, UK CA3 0QS

Production and Printing in England by
Nuprint Ltd, Station Road, Harpenden, Herts, AL5 4SE.

CONTENTS

CHAIRMAN'S INTRODUCTION

At Keswick there is always something new. This year the platform was adorned by a very attractive collage which visualised the theme of our week 'The Cross and the Crown'. This new idea of having a title to undergird the unchanging Keswick message has real value. The simple challenge of our theme this year was not just that we go through the cross to the crown. It was a reminder that there is always a cost in following the One who is victorious but who wore a crown of thorns.

The theme was suggested by our two Bible Readings and as often our expositors blended styles beautifully. It is significant that preaching can be equally effective but with diverse gifts and moulds of preaching. Raymond Brown's exposition of the Passion narratives had a lot of heart in it but of course it came with great academic integrity. Derick Bingham with his delightful Ulster style and accent expounded the book of Esther in a very different way but with tremendous power.

I encourage students of preaching to study the two different expositions and to discover how equally effective they can be while coming in very different ways. Putting together the two Bible Readings reminds us that we too are called to the world of today with a challenge to take up the cross and follow Jesus. We are asked at some cost to make our witness to the risen victorious Lord.

It was, I believe, very relevant that this year we had in our speaker team so many different links with the worldwide church and ministry with George Hoffman, Chua Wee Hiang and Tom Houston in particular. In every way we could not forget that the joy of Christian Fellowship around God's word and the beauty of Keswick is only the prelude to going back into a very dark world with much sin and sorrow, and, like Esther, daring to make our witness—even like Jesus going all the way to Calvary so that there might be the glory of resurrection. It was a very powerful Keswick, a week of great joy and yet one where always we are reminded that there is a price to pay in Christian obedience and holiness.

Philip Hacking
Chairman of the Keswick Convention Council

EDITOR'S INTRODUCTION

The key word that struck your editor this year was 'context'; both in a global sense, as speaker after speaker applied the word of God to issues and crises ranging from the Barcelona Olympics to the various theatres of war in the current world, and in a Convention sense, as not only was there the usual interplay of ideas and insight between speakers (Malchus' ear was a recurring theme, for example), but there was a strong sense of the wider Keswick audience, sharing in the ministry often thousands of miles away from the familiar tent in Skiddaw Street. For that reason, in fact, I have placed Derick Bingham's Bible Readings first in the volume, though they were given in the second week: his constant direct comments to the book, video and tape audience made such an arrangement the obvious way to start. If you were not able to attend the Keswick Convention in person in 1992, this book is by no means a poor consolation.

It does, however, contain only part of what was said: all the Bible Readings and a selection of the addresses, chosen by the Keswick Council and abridged to retain as much as possible of the teaching. This means that as usual, some instructive anecdotes, excellent illustrations and extremely funny jokes have had to go. Recently we produced an anthology, *Keswick Gold*,[1] which contained a selection of vintage Keswick exposition. In a recession-free world there might be a good case for a *Keswick Anecdotes and Illustrations* anthology. However, even in the present economic climate, those who would like to have the complete text will find inexpensive and efficient tape and video libraries described on pp. 219-220.

The texts have been transcribed (this year by Anthony Watson and my wife Tricia) and then edited. To publish by Christmas involves a tight schedule which means that the speakers rarely have the opportunity to revise the edited text. Please keep in mind, therefore, that what you have in this book is the transcript of a spoken Convention. Bible references have been checked (against the version each speaker used) but often abridged, so an open Bible by your side as you read will be extremely useful. Where a speaker has paraphrased, I have preserved his (often creative) variations and added 'cf' to the reference. In exact quotations the punctuation of the original is followed, so where pronouns referring to the Persons of the Trinity are capitalised it means the speaker was paraphrasing.

I would like to add my personal farewell to Maurice Rowlandson, Secretary of the Convention, who retires this year; his geniality and friendliness have made the enjoyable task of editing even more enjoyable for me over the years. Dave Brown, OM's publishing director for the fifteen years I have been involved with this book, has also moved on, to bookshop management. It has been a hugely enjoyable partnership for me, and has included some very satisfying Keswick mountain-top experiences in a most literal sense.

David Porter

Note

1. David Porter (ed.), *Keswick Gold: Outstanding Messages from Recent Keswick Conventions* (OM Publishing, 1990).

THE BIBLE READINGS

'For such a Time as This': Studies in the Book of Esther

by Mr Derick Bingham

1. Can You be Beautiful without being Good-Looking? (Esther 1:1–2:20)

Welcome to all of you joining us by means of tape recordings, video and the printed page—across the world, round the corner, up the road, wherever you may be. Welcome to Keswick! May the Lord bless these messages to your heart, wherever you are listening, reading and watching. We are considering this morning the first chapter and most of the second chapter of the Book of Esther.

There is no question but that God brings about unbelievable endings from uneventful beginnings. And what could be more uneventful than the beginning of this amazing book? 'And it came to pass'—or as the New International Version has it, 'This is what happened'. It seems a very lack-lustre beginning. What seems very mundane to you and me this morning in our lives may simply be the preparation for something monumental. The Chairman of this Convention said last evening that what excited him about the Convention was the potential in these great meetings, day after day; and with all my heart I believe this to be a historic moment in your life and in mine. I come to this Convention anticipating that our God is going to do mighty things in thousands of lives, through the ministry of the word of God through this very special two weeks. There is no telling what God may do. That's why I find Christian work so exciting.

Louis Palau has said the greatest temptation in his life as a great Christian evangelist (he wouldn't so describe himself, but we would) is the desire to quit, because we feel so useless, so empty in ourselves, so unable for these things. And Christians get discouraged and they get down and they get disheartened. Christian, if there's anything I want to do through the word of God and the power of the Spirit at the very beginning of this week, it is to encourage you. You love the Lord Jesus; you are His child; you are unique. The Lord wants and wills to use you. And as the great Harold St John, father of the great writer Patricia St John, said, 'Walk in the conscious knowledge that you are beloved of the Lord.' The devil wants you to live like a pauper. He wants to strip you of everything you have in Christ. He wants you to feel this morning that indeed, you cannot be used of God. But we are here to tell you again from the word of God that although you may feel your life mundane and very ordinary, there is no such a thing in the world as an 'ordinary person'.

I was recently expounding the 139th psalm. I asked a friend of mine, a gynaecological surgeon, 'Will you come and give me a crash course on the baby in the womb?' And he came to my house with his medical books and described to me the growth of a baby in the womb. I shall never forget it. I can't remember all the statistics now but they were just incredible. When a child in the womb is one three-hundredths of an inch it has, as I understand it, all the foundation of its nervous system in place.

Somebody rang me up recently. 'I want to have an abortion, Derick.'

I said, 'Is there anything wrong with your child?'

'No,' she said, 'I'm a born-again believer.'

I said, 'You're a born-again believer and you want to have an abortion? What does your husband think?'

'He says it's up to me.'

I never thought I would live to see the day when I would have to plead for a little one's life on the phone. But she said, 'It's only a tiny little thing.' I said, 'Have you any idea of the wonder of that little one, even when it's only one three-hundredths of an inch?' And I started to describe it to her.

I said, 'What is your name?'

She said, 'I don't want to tell you what my name is.' No wonder!

The beauty of it, the wonder of it! David, long before there were scanners, long before we had all the medical knowledge we have now, wrote that all our members are written down in God's book (Psa. 139:16). Whether you would be right-handed or left-handed; whether you'd be blue-eyed or brown-eyed; whether you'd have a whole lot of hair or very little hair; whether you would be tall or small—all those details.

Oh Christian! In Christ's name we plead with you this morning! See your position in Christ! Walk in the conscious knowledge that you are beloved of the Lord and that God has a mighty work for you to do. And we'll see that, morning by morning, in this amazing story. Uneventful, mundane, seemingly ordinary—but about to become monumental. When you come into Christ you are into the biggest restoration programme in all of the universe. You're enjoying this meeting, aren't you? The fellowship of saints at Keswick? Well—to borrow a phrase from President Reagan—'You ain't seen nothing, yet!' You're on the edge of a vast adventure that is only beginning. You're only starting. Look what's up ahead; the coming of the Lord draws nigh, you're about to see a new heaven and a new earth! And if this one is so wonderful, what is the new one going to be like? So don't just glance at that first verse. In it is the seed-bed of the monumental providence of God in the life of this amazing woman. What follows is anything but dull.

Here at the beginning we have a party. What a party! It lasted for 180 days. The aristocracy attended, and then they had a party for ordinary folk, in Susa (in Greek) which is Shushan (in Hebrew). Notice the description of this wonderful place in verse 6—what a set-up! The king, right in the middle of this long, long feast that lasted about six months (imagine a Keswick Convention six months long) became inebriated, and he ordered Queen Vashti to come before him with her royal crown, in order to show her beauty to the people—for, says the Scripture, she was beautiful to behold. And she said 'No. I'm not coming.'

Now, great argument rages around her behaviour. Some say that she should have thought about the consequences of her actions, that her refusal might cause a scandal that would damage her husband. 'I'm very sorry, gentlemen, but we'll have to change our programme for the evening'—because of all this going on behind the scenes. Can you imagine the embarrassment? The guests might begin to say, 'What kind of a king is he that cannot even command his queen?' And that wouldn't be good, some thought, for the stability of this empire.

What he did was contrary to the custom of Persia, because the women customarily feasted apart from the men. Why did she refuse? Was she right? The answer for me is found in the very wise words of the great Alexander Whyte, the Scots preacher. He said, 'Whatever the royal order that came to her out of the banqueting hall was, the brave queen refused to obey it. Her beauty was her own and her husband's. It was not for open show among hundreds of half-drunk men.'

What she did started a huge national debate on women's rights, that led to an edict regarding marriages in the Median-Persian empire. And up speaks Memucan there in verse 16. He certainly seems to have been a hen-pecked husband, if ever there was one. He is afraid that when the queen's deed comes to the attention of all women they will look with contempt upon their husbands. The king's edict said that Vashti should no longer come into the king's presence, that her position was going to be given to someone else and that all women should give honour to their husband.

Here's a problem. Ephesians 5:22-24 teaches categorically that a Christian wife should submit to her husband. But how many times have battered wives beaten by drunken husbands come to me and say, 'What do I do?' Do you think, Christian, that this teaching of a wife submitting to her husband is an absolute command without limits? It's certainly an absolute command—but without limits? I want to say solemnly this morning that a woman does not have to give up her dignity as a human being when she becomes a wife. Neither should she allow her principles to be trodden underfoot by an unprincipled husband. Let me quote a great Ulsterman, C. S. Lewis: 'Marriage does not give the husband licence to pursue his basest sexual fantasies, and neither does it enslave the wife to fulfil them.'

Are you listening, sir? How do you treat your wife? Are

you sir, a sexual slob? Ask anybody involved in Christian
work: the biggest problem we face at the moment is the
breakdown of Christian marriages on an epidemic scale. Virtually every week I have to deal with it. We are bombarded
with erotic material from selling cars to selling perfume—you
name it. If you switch your television off it'll wink at you out
of the Sunday colour supplements, it'll come at you from
radio, it's everywhere! It is pouring across this nation. A
woman is treated as an object, to be lifted and led according
to a man's desire. The Scripture abhors it! Christ lifted a
woman and set her on a plane that no-one has ever done
before or since. You do not have to fulfil those sexual fantasies of that sexual slob, if that's what he is, just because
you're a Christian.

I support Vashti. She didn't have to parade before those
drunken men. That's not what beauty is created for. To have
and to hold a woman's love is a lifetime's work. It's not
something to be lifted and led according to how you feel. So
Ahasuerus divorces Vashti. Yet all of those circumstances
made way for Esther. God overruled.

Let's make a very careful distinction here. God didn't
make Ahasuerus drunk. God didn't put into his heart that
unholy desire to manipulate the fabulous beauty of his wife
before his drunken friends. But God was in the shadows
while Ahasuerus and his crowd of lords indulged in their
carousal. While Vashti declines to yield to the whim of the
king, God uses Esther for the deliverance.

Recently I was at Radio Ulster taking part in a radio
phone-in programme. In the middle of it the presenter said to
me, 'Derick, what about Judas? Isn't it predicted in the Bible
that he would do what he did?'

'Yes,' I agreed. 'It's stated categorically, in the psalms.'

'Then,' he said, 'there wasn't anything that he could do,
really, was there?'

Well, it's true that the word of God says clearly that
somebody would betray Christ, and would buy a field with
the proceeds, as Acts tells us Judas did, and that the field
would be left desolate. Nobody's lived in it ever since; it's a
cemetery to this day. But Judas had a free choice. He could
have chosen not to deny Christ, not to betray Him. God was

not pushing and pushing in His sovereign will, pushing Israel to crucify His Son—pushing the leaders of Israel. If there are any Jewish friends here this morning, can I say to you that you're most welcome; and that my sins were as responsible for putting Jesus on the cross as any other's sin. We as evangelicals are not coming to you as a threat. I've been reading all those letters in *The Times* over the past few months as you have been reacting to the 'decade of evangelism' and your view of evangelism and so forth. We are here in gentile territory, and our sins put the Saviour on the cross as much as anybody else's. We too are guilty. But God was not pushing the religious leaders of that time and manipulating them to crucify Christ. They chose to do so.

So Ahasuerus chooses to divorce this woman, but God comes in and overrules in His providence, in this situation. People decide and act for themselves but they fulfil Jehovah's wonderful overruling, power and will, as much as the sun and the moon and the stars. His very enemies, in opposing Him, are made the instruments of serving Him. When you look around and you see everywhere people trampling on God's laws and openly dishonouring Him, God isn't disappointed and overcome by the prince of darkness. No, the Lord is executing His purposes even through the wickedness of men and devils. He doesn't use evil, He overrules it. God works all things according to the counsel of His own will. Christian, everything that happens to you is not necessarily good, but it always works together for good. Always.

And of course Ahasuerus now gets lonely and is looking for a new queen. His men devise a plan whereby every beautiful girl in the kingdom is brought to Susa, the capital. Cosmetics are given to them (2:3) and the king prepares to choose. Now, a young Jewess named Esther, raised by her cousin, totally obscure, has been given a gift of beauty. Notice there's a miracle wrought here by God, a miracle as surprising as the very preservation of Israel itself. Many of those employed to effect it were as ignorant of God as the king of Persia was. But could anybody be so blind as not to perceive that it was entirely providential, that of the small number of captive Jews in that vast area there should be found this beautiful girl, more beautiful than any other young

woman, in an empire that stretched from India to Ethiopia—
127 provinces? Could anybody question that God gave her
that exquisite loveliness for this very purpose? If God hadn't
given her that beauty, surpassing all others, the previous
events would have been useless. When He created Esther,
God had an eye to the plan which He intended to execute
through her. She was found the most beautiful woman, so
that her beauty might be used by God to deliver the people of
God.

So what have we learned from this first chapter? Charles
Swindoll summed it up for me perfectly when he said, 'God's
plans are not hindered when events are secular and carnal.'
You say, 'I have an unconverted husband', 'I have teenagers
who are breaking my heart', 'I go home from Keswick, it's
like heaven for me here, but Derick, you want to see what it's
like at home for me, when I come down out of this wonderful
time, down into the reality of everyday life, and it's secular
and it's carnal—all the music is secular, all the language is
carnal language.' Oh Christian, God's plans are not hindered
when events are secular and carnal.

I've just been in Eastern Europe, and you only have to
travel there to see that God overrules. In Romania I stood in
a printer's workshop on the boulevard that Ceausescu had
built—all those fabulous apartments for the party faithful. A
seventy-nine year old man there told me, 'I feel young since I
came here. That Heidelberg printing press came from a
Christian press set up by Pastor Wurmbrand in the very
apartment where he was beaten up by the security forces
years before. We bought the press off the East German
communist propaganda office, and we're printing Christian
books on it.'

I said, 'Brother, what do you put it down to?'

I can still see the twinkle in his eye as in his broken English
accent he said, 'He that sitteth in ze heavens shall laugh!'

And I went outside and looked at that monstrosity of a
palace with 7,000 rooms. I'd just dined with a little old
Christian lady in her lovely old home, but it just missed being
flattened because it was near where Ceausescu was building
his palace. Seven thousand rooms—all with no purpose.
They have a book in the palace you can write in. It simply

asks, 'What would you like this palace used for? Give us a suggestion. A prison? A hospital?' I could almost hear, and I speak reverently, God, laughing up and down that ridiculous monument to man's vanity. God's plans are not hindered when events are carnal.

Neither are God's purposes frustrated by marital or moral conflicts. The Lord had a plan prepared for the deliverance of His people even before their enemies had prepared the plot for their destruction. How did He do it? With a beautiful woman. What were the characteristics of Esther? Well, she had a lot of perfume, that's for sure. An old lady asked me one day on a Belfast street when I was walking with my daughter Kerry: 'Derick, what do you think? Should a Christian woman wear make-up?' I was in the middle of traffic and I was supposed to give an answer to this profound theological problem.

I drew a breath—as I do this morning!—and said, 'There are two views on this. There's the W. P. Nicholson view; he stood up in a meeting and said, 'Would all the women in this congregation who do not use make-up put their hands up.' And all these godly women raised their hands; and Nicholson, powerful wild man he was, said, 'Ladies, it's a poor old barn door that doesn't improve with a lick of paint.' That rocked the evangelicals of Ulster! But before you panic and think I'm teaching the 'Nicholson line', let me give you the other view of make-up:

> Dare to be a Daniel,
> dare to stand alone,
> dare to pass the chemist's shop
> and call your face your own.

It's a controversial issue!

I'm told that Esther saturated her hair and the pores of her skin with fumes from cosmetic burners. Any woman will tell you that the best way to apply perfume is to spray it. Six months with oil of myrrh, six months with perfume (2:12). Amazing, isn't it? A lot of women sometimes think that perfume can really make you; I read a perfume advertisement the other day that claimed the perfume was 'witty,

confident, devastatingly feminine.' How could a perfume be
witty? But they were serious.

Did Esther's qualities lie in the perfume she lived with?
No. Did the beauty of this woman, and her greatness which
God used, come from all that make-up and perfume? No!
The Scriptures teach that it isn't outward adornment that
makes you beautiful. It is what you are, within. You can be
beautiful, Christian, without being good-looking. Some
people who are not physically endowed by any means, and
whom many would call ugly, are among the most beautiful
Christians I know. Nor do you need to have cosmetics, beautiful dresses or lovely suits to make you beautiful. Ask
George Hoffman, whom God has used so mightily amongst
the poor of the world; ask him where he has met the most
beautiful Christians. He'll tell you, 'In some of the poorest
places in the world'. I'll never forget him talking, in my own
pulpit in Belfast, about the song that was written to raise
relief funds, 'Do they know it's Christmas?'. George pointed
out that in the heart of Ethiopia, a country for which much of
the aid was intended, there exists one of the greatest Christian churches that he has ever come across in the world. 'Do
they know it's Christmas?' They could show us the way.

What were her qualities? Verse 9 says literally that 'she
lifted up grace before his face'. When this man took her into
the harem she exuded grace and beauty in the presence of
others. Secondly, it's very clear that this lady had verbal
restraint. She didn't tell them she was a Jewess. There is a
time to speak, and a time to refrain from speaking; she knew
the moment when to say and the moment when not to say.
Thirdly, she showed in verses 10 and 20 that she had a
continually teachable spirit; becoming a finalist before
becoming a queen didn't go to her head. What a lovely
quality! And she had a student's spirit, a willingness to listen
and learn. Have you? I think you have, because you're here
to hear the word this week.

Some of the worst-behaved people in the Bible—Samson,
David, and more—had the greatest gifts; and some people
who have very few gifts could show the very gifted the way.
Just because you're gifted doesn't mean to say you always use
your gift in a godly way. Be careful if you are highly gifted,

my brother, my sister, to give your Lord the glory, and to have a teachable spirit.

She was unselfishly modest (2:12-14). Let loose in Harrod's and given a free rein to take whatever cosmetics and clothes you wanted, what would you do? Esther was offered all the jewellery from the show-cases, all the cosmetic products, all free! But she didn't take advantage of it, did she? Certainly not. She was so wise, the Scripture tells us. 'She obtained grace and favour' (2:17) but she requested nothing but what Hegai advised her. She had a winsomeness, despite her surroundings.

As I close, can I just underline it all? Listen to this verse:

> The church throughout all Judaea and Galilee and Samaria enjoyed peace. Being built up and going on in the fear of the Lord and in the comfort of the Holy Spirit, it continued to increase.

Where do you read those lovely words, about a church that is blossoming and going forward powerfully? I'll tell you. Acts 9:31. The Christians were being flogged, persecuted, threatened, warned by the warring people around them, the Jewish community, Nero the emperor and all the rest of it. And instead of shrivelling up into a camp of bitter and frightened people they remained winsome and magnetic. I love this quotation, though I do not know where it comes from:

> You may be able to compel people to maintain certain minimum standards by stressing duty, but the highest moral and spiritual achievements depend not upon a push—but a pull.

A pull in your life so lovely that they say 'What has that fellow got? What has that girl got?' Let's have a return to— excuse the phrase—Christian charm. Show me a negative congregation and I'll show you a negative preacher. How are you being fed, how are we feeding you, on the loveliness that is in Christ?

A little boy was carrying a jigsaw along a Manhattan sidewalk. The crowd was thronging to the subway, and he was knocked over and his jigsaw scattered all over the ground. The man who had knocked him over ran on a few paces, then stopped in his tracks and turned back to where the little boy was. He got down beside him, pulled all the jigsaw bits together from under people's feet, and put them all back into the box.

The little lad looked at him, in the middle of that mayhem, and he said: 'Tell me, Sir; is your name Jesus?'

2. Can the Insignificant be Significant? (Esther 2:21–4:17)

Halfway through chapter 2 you might think that you could anticipate an idyllic ending. Esther, a beautiful young woman, is married to a famous king. It's a happy-ever-after situation. But in fact Esther was called to walk, just as you and I are often called in our own walk with God, down a very dark alley. As I said yesterday, it's so good to have many of you watching us by video, listening to tapes and reading the Keswick ministry, all around the world; but as you are watching, listening or reading at this moment—perhaps reading in hospital, listening while driving a car, watching us in your own home or church—you may be going through a very dark patch, walking down a very dark alley in your life too.

In 2:21-22 a secret conspiracy forms. Two men rise up, the doorkeepers Bigthan and Teresh, seeking to assassinate King Ahasuerus. Word of the plot is leaked to Mordecai and from him, through Esther, to the king; the insurgents are hanged. So first of all there is a conspiracy against Esther's husband. Here we have the intrusion of suffering, but it doesn't end there. Esther next moves into a time of even deeper suffering, because this time the trouble comes from higher up; not from the door-keepers in the palace but from Haman himself, up the official ladder. Trouble comes from within the very inner court of this great king. And Haman, this man who had hatred in his heart against the Jewish people, is

23

promoted. Mordecai—whom you would think would have been honoured by the king for saving his life—is overlooked.

I had a friend who happened to be fishing in the same bay when Lord Mountbatten was so cruelly assassinated. He helped to take some of those bodies from the water. I was in his house a while back, and there was a lovely portrait of Queen Elizabeth which she had signed. He was so proud of that picture. He had simply done what he could in that situation, but he had not been overlooked by the sovereign. You can imagine how Mordecai felt, when this man who was so rotten and evil was promoted over his head. And maybe, dear Christian, today, you have lived for your Lord; you have served in your business or school or university or wherever—and people who don't love the Lord and have no time for the Scriptures or the things of God have been promoted over your head; and you are discouraged. Think of Mordecai, in this situation.

Haman was a descendent of Agag the Amalekite. The Amelekites were the first enemy to attack Israel after Egypt, for which God decreed they should be punished by continual war and ultimate obliteration. Saul refused to carry that out, and he was himself slain by an Amelekite. Mordecai refused to pay homage to Haman: for a Jew to bow down in that way would have been an act of idolatry. And out of Haman's wicked heart came this incredibly sad and vile plot for the extermination of all the Jews in that great empire. It is, without question, holocaust thinking, it is genocide: 'It is not fitting for the king to let them remain' (3:8).

The king had so little regard for human life he didn't even enquire who the people were that Haman wanted to exterminate. Think of the cruelty of that! Haman was going to confiscate all the property of the Jews, estimated at 375 tons of silver and two-thirds of the annual income of the entire Persian empire. What is the king's attitude? 'I don't know who they are and I don't care, but if you feel they should be exterminated, Haman, then go ahead and take care of the matter.' What incredible callousness!

The announcement goes out. It took a great effort because this empire stretched from India all the way down through the fertile crescent and the Mediterranean, through Egypt to

Ethiopia. In it were people speaking 127 languages and tribes speaking all kinds of dialects within that. The edict had to be translated into a lot of tongues, and then be taken out by courier to every corner of the empire. It proclaimed that on the thirteenth day of the twelfth month every Jew, man, woman and child was to be killed. Think about that. It is anti-Semitism at its height, at full rein, permitting a great many people to do what apparently was in their hearts to do. On a designated day in that empire, it would be legal to kill a Jew. We are told that Haman and the king sat down to drink. But the city of Shushan was perplexed. The Jews were not traitors, they had committed no great crime. Why such extreme measures against these people? They could not understand the king permitting an edict like this.

It might have worried the people but it certainly didn't worry the king and Haman. Anti-Semitism is an awful thing. It started in the brickyards of Egypt and it has carried on down, even through Saddam Hussein and the rise of neo-Nazism in Germany at the present time. Why has there always been such incredible hatred of the Jewish people? Churchill's secretary, Martin Gilbert—himself a Jew—has written a brilliant book cataloguing the events of the holocaust.[1] I had to stop reading it, it was so distressing, I couldn't sleep at night. Gilbert indicates that even some devout Christians have gone astray in this area. What they have done is to treat all Jews as Christ-killers, which is something the Bible does not do. Hitler rode on that kind of feeling: in Germany in his day there was anti-Jewish feeling even in some Christian quarters.

In the early church the Jews persecuted the Christians. But sadly, when the Emperor Constantine became a Christian and it was the done thing to be a Christian, many Christians rose up and used their status quo to persecute the Jews. You and I abhor it with all our hearts. I heard of an evangelist recently who stood up before a large congregation in Britain and pleaded with them to come to Christ. 'Because if you don't,' he said, 'look what happened to the Jews when they didn't: the Holocaust.'

That's not biblical teaching. That's horrific.

Lord Jakobovits, former Chief Rabbi of Great Britain,

was interviewed by Terry Wogan on television. He was asked, 'Why have the Jews been persecuted so greatly through the generations? Why do people hate you so much?'

He said something I have never forgotten. 'It is dislike of the unlike.'

You see, God chose those people. There was that great tabernacle set up in the wilderness with its fabulous gold, its linen fence, its 'holy of holies'. And as that tabernacle, so strange to the people around it, passed through the wilderness the people were saying: 'Who do these people think they are with their "holy of holies"? Do they think they're the only ones going to heaven? That they hold a monopoly on truth?' And they hated them, because the Jewish people were chosen to represent the glory of God. Always remember, friends, that when in Britain people were running round painted blue and black in a very unsophisticated culture, the Jewish people were representing the glory of God.

That's why people have always hated them. Because they are different. That's why, of course, people hate the church of Jesus Christ; why even in universities I find great opposition when I stand up and claim that there is one mediator between God and man, the man Christ Jesus. To say that in many circles at the moment would be deemed anti-social. Young folk, this is the great problem you're going to have to face sooner or later. This is why at Keswick we want to encourage you in these services, we want to feed you on the word of God. Because at your universities and colleges and schools, you will have to stand up for your belief that when Jesus said 'I am the way, the truth and the life, no man cometh unto the Father but by Me', He meant it. And you're going to be considered, as a lady considered me once, very unchristian. 'You're very unchristian,' she said, 'because you say Jesus is the only way.' But Jesus said it first!

You're going to have to face this. I'm facing it all the time. And you'll be persecuted for it, just like the early Christians were. Just remember that when the early Christians stood up and preached the glory of the Messiah all the Old Testament prophesied for it was only a shadow of the substance. It was pointing to the Lamb of God who bears away the sin of the world. Jesus didn't come to condemn the law, He came to fulfil it. And of course the church of Jesus Christ witnessed to the Lord Jesus. If the church of Jesus Christ in the New Testament had given up the things that liberals are asking us now to give up in the historic Christian faith; if they had given them up in order to accommodate the multi-culture of religions around them—there wouldn't have been a Christian church in the first place. There would have been no teaching on the resurrection, the efficacy of the precious blood of Christ to save, the second coming of Christ and so forth.

O Christian, let's not be ashamed of our unique and lovely Lord—let us proclaim Him! It wasn't that the Christians in the early church didn't recognise that there were other religions around them. It was as much 'New Age' then as it is now. Professor Wiseman has said, 'There is no century which is more like the first century than the twentieth century.' We're going right back to astrology (dished up to us on television every morning), and looking to the stars in the nation for guidance. When the gospel came sweeping through New Testament times, even into Nero's very palace, people who had looked to the astrologers were set free from all that terrible slavery. But we're going right back to it. No, it wasn't that the early church didn't recognise there were other religions. It was because so many gods were proclaimed that they saw the beauty and the glory of the one, true and only Saviour, and witnessed to Him.

But they suffered for it. And now Esther is about to suffer, because of the people she belongs to, because of what they stand for.

This is not an easy subject to teach, and I want to tackle it head on. I'd like to recommend to you in passing the chapter on suffering in a book from which I have received a great deal of help—John Stott's *The Cross of Christ*[2]—so much so, in fact, that I want to acknowledge its help in this difficult area. He cites the great earthquake of November 1755 in Lisbon in Portugal. The city was devastated. Thirty churches were destroyed, all full of people. Within six minutes 15,000 people died and 15,000 more were dying. And Voltaire, the great French atheist, demanded, 'How could anybody now believe in the benevolence and omnipotence of God?' He asked this great question: 'If God is free, just and beneficent, why do we have to suffer under His rule?' That's the old conundrum isn't it? Either God is not good or He's not almighty. Either He wants to stop suffering but cannot, or He could stop it but will not. How many of you Christians have faced that question from unconverted people? 'Why does God allow suffering?'

Why does this lovely girl Esther, with all her qualities of character, have to face a holocaust of all her people in which it would be legal to kill them? 'How can we worship such a God?' say the unconverted. I am told that in Ethiopia, at the height of the drought for which Bob Geldof and others did such a great job to raise relief, some missionaries were almost losing their faith. Yet the evolutionists were saying, 'Well, you win some and you lose some'; the existentialists were saying, 'Life doesn't have any meaning, there is no meaning in life whatsoever'; many people didn't see the drought as a problem. They said, 'That's the way it is: droughts come, droughts go.' But you and I as believers have a problem with it, because we believe there's a loving hand behind this universe and that life has a meaning.

You see, the problem of suffering is far from one that only troubles philosophers. It impinges on all of us. Is there a girl sitting here this morning—and I want to speak tenderly—who is saying 'I can't stand singleness'? Christian preachers make such a great thing of marriage. What about those of us who will never be married? What's the meaning of that? Maybe you're a teenager sitting here this morning with a broken love affair. Those of us who are older so often say the usual things—'There's more fish in the sea'—and all that nonsense. But it's real to the teenager! It is breaking their heart, it is the biggest thing in their life. Maybe you're a teenager like that this morning, and your heart is breaking. Maybe you sit here this morning with a very unhappy marriage. Maybe you sit here this morning divorced. Maybe there are many here deeply depressed and lonely in a great crowd. Maybe you have a chronic illness. Maybe you're in a dead-end career. You are facing suffering, just as Esther is about to face incredible suffering, and you ask 'Why?' and you ask, 'Why me?'

I tell you folks, if you prayed in your local church prayer meeting like Job prayed, the elders would say to you, 'Don't pray next week like that please.' Let me paraphrase his prayer. 'Lord, it's not those who don't love You who are firing arrows at me—it's You!' Joseph Parker of the City Temple, London's great preacher, lost his wife at the age of sixty-eight. He said, 'I became almost an atheist, for God had set His foot upon my prayers and treated my petitions with contempt, and if I had seen a dog in such agony as mine I would have pitied and helped the dumb animal. Yet God spat upon me and cast me out as an offence, out into the waste wilderness and the night black and starless.' And that's one of the great classical evangelical preachers.

What has the Bible got to say? Well, John Stott says that the Bible supplies no thorough solution to the problem of evil, whether in the form of suffering or sin. Notice his phraseology—'thorough solution'. Its purpose, he says (and I find this helpful) is more practical than philosophical. You ask, why does God allow evil? Why did God allow Hitler? Why does God allow a Saddam Hussein? Why did God allow a Haman? Why does God allow that person to persecute you? I once had to break the news of a great tragedy to a dear lady. It's the hardest thing I've ever had to do. She asked me, 'What have we done wrong?' But she hadn't done anything wrong.

David asked Jonathan, 'What have I done? Why is your father persecuting me?' (1 Sam 20:1) . And Jonathan had to say, 'You haven't done anything, David. Basically, God has allowed this to happen.' And I think John Stott's argument is helpful when you think about it. God's dealing with evil and suffering is more practical than philosophical in the Bible. Consequently, although there are references to sin and suffering on virtually every page of the Bible, its concern is not to explain their origin but to help us overcome them.

According to the Bible, firstly suffering is an alien intrusion into God's good world and will have no part in the new universe; and secondly, suffering is often due to sin, which is how disease and death entered the world. Sometimes it's the sin of others, as when children suffer from irresponsible parents, the poor and hungry from economic injustice, refugees from the cruelties of war, road victims from drunken drivers. At other times suffering can be caused by the consequence of our own sin, yet the Bible firmly repudiates the dreadful Hindu doctrine of Karma, which attributes all suffering to wrongdoing in this or a previous existence. That's not true! If you're a Hindu friend here this morning please, please, thank you for coming or watching. We love you, but we want—as the Archbishop said at his enthronement—'to listen to your story, but then we want to bring the claims of the unique and lovely Lord Jesus to you.' And the claim of the Lord Jesus and the teaching of His word is that not all suffering in our life is because of sin.

It's believed that Job had the skin disease elephantiasis, putrid breath, and insomnia. He had death in his family, lost his business and lost his position as an elder in the land. He sat among the rubbish, outside the city, and his three friends came to him to encourage him. Job's comforters. Their theology, though there's some good things in it, is basically this: 'God is good to the good and He's bad to the bad; and Job, you must have sinned, or you wouldn't have all this suffering.' But that's not true. Job has now discovered in heaven that he was a witness between the hosts of heaven and the legions of hell, as a man who could have affection and love for God even though he got nothing out of it materially or physically. 'Though He slay me yet will I trust Him' (Job 13:15).

Of course suffering is sometimes due to human sensitivity to pain. When you and I go through trouble, we have physical and emotional reactions. Nerves have to hurt if we are to protect ourselves. But is suffering meaningless? Is all this in the Book of Esther meaningless? Is there no purpose whatever to be detected in it? No. Why? Because the Lord Jesus spoke in John 9:3 about a man blind from birth. 'Neither has this man nor his parents sinned, but that the works of God should be revealed in him.'

Who knows what a day may bring forth for you and for me, what kind of a year it will be between this Keswick and the next? I live in Belfast, a city and a province of haunting but tragic beauty. I hear bombs go off virtually every night of my life. I was away preaching the other night and when I came home my wife told me, 'A bomb went off in a hotel just

down the road, and our bed lifted clean off the ground.'
We've had twenty years of it since I left university. Is there
meaning to it? I think of my friend David Lennox in Armagh,
he runs a department store right in the centre. They've
threatened to burn him out—I'll not go into the details. A
bomb went off and dear David's eye was badly damaged. I
went to see him. He'd lost twelve pints of blood in a few
minutes. A friend of mine lifted him off the ground, stopped
a passing lorry, put him in the back, got him to hospital and
saved his life. I said, 'David, what is it like?'

He said, 'Derick, if God can bring order out of the chaos
of the cross He can bring order out of the chaos of my face.'

The cross of Christ rises again in this convention. Esther
has a crown, yes; but I tell you she has a cross to bear. What
does the cross say to us this morning? It is a stimulus to us, to
patient endurance of our suffering. 'He endured the cross,'
say the Scriptures, 'despising the shame' (Heb. 12:1). He left
us an example for us to follow in His steps. We go into deep
territory here.

> For it was fitting for him, for whom are all things and by whom
> are all things, in bringing many sons to glory, to make the author
> of their salvation perfect through sufferings. (Heb. 2:10)

The author of our salvation, perfect—through what? Sufferings.

If the Lord Jesus suffered, do you think you're going to
escape? Do you think I'm going to escape? 'Though he was a
son, yet he learned obedience by the things which he suffered. And having been perfected, he became the author of
eternal salvation to all who obey him' (Heb. 5:8). Learned
obedience by the things that He suffered? You don't think,
do you, that you and I should be joyous and happy, laughing
and smiling all the time? That's not what the Bible teaches.
Jesus wept.

> For the law appoints as high priests men who have weakness, but
> the word of the oath, which came after the law, appoints the Son
> who has been perfected for ever. (Heb. 7:28)

How? By suffering. Ah, but notice the qualification the

writer makes in 4:15, 'For we do not have a high priest who cannot sympathise with our weaknesses, but was in all points tempted as we are, yet without sin.' He suffered, He learned obedience, He was perfected—but He was sinless. There's a mystery. He was never disobedient, but His sufferings were the testing ground in which His obedience became full grown. And you and I will suffer, like Esther suffered. But joy will come in the morning like it does in the Book of Esther. 'My brethren, count it all joy when you fall into various trials, knowing that the testing of your faith produces patience. But let patience have its perfect work, that you may be perfect [fully mature] and complete, lacking nothing' (Jas. 1:2-4). 'Before I was afflicted' said David, 'I went astray, but now I keep your word' (Psa. 119:67). What an incredible, wonderful theme.

And now Esther faces it head on. 'If I go in before the king, I'm going to die if he doesn't lift his golden sceptre to me' (4:11). 'Does it really matter whether I go in or not? If he doesn't lift it to me, I'll perish.'

Mordecai pleading so powerfully with her—what an incredible argument he uses! 'If you do nothing they'll find out anyway that you're a Jew, Esther, and you will be destroyed'—though the Jewish race will survive and deliverance will arise 'from another place' (4:14). God has promised His people He'll bring them through, just like He has promised the Christian church that the gates of hell will not prevail against it. We will win, and Christ will reign, even though we go through seas of suffering.

What are you going to do? You say, 'But what am I among so many?' 150,000,000 malnourished under-fives in the world. 7,000,000 war refugees. 100,000,000 children who will never enter a classroom. 30,000,000 children in our world live in the streets; 10,000,000 in Africa alone will have lost at least one parent to AIDS by the year 2000; 40,000 children will die every day. It's easy to get lost among the statistics, to look at all the confusion in the world and say 'What can I do? What difference can I make? I'm only a drop in the ocean.' But you can make a difference; one, with God, is a majority. What you might think is insignificant can be very significant.

On a recent visit to Madame Tussaud's I saw two Japanese young people looking at a model of a little man with a pock-marked face. They approached me and asked me who he was. 'That's William Wilberforce,' I said.

'Who was Wilberforce?' they asked. I explained how Wilberforce campaigned against slavery for thirty-five years, and saw the Bill for the Abolition of Slavery passed only a few weeks before he died. He was said to be ugly and ungainly, but that little man, who was converted through reading Paul's letter to the Romans, rid the British Empire of one of the darkest blots on its history. One man, determined to do something.

Look at England, look at Europe, slipping back; Scotland going secular, the problems in Ulster. Can you and I make a difference? Yes! We can—in the Lord's hands. Esther stood up and was counted.

Moses stood before God and pleaded. God had made a covenant with the people. He said, 'If you break it I'll scatter you, I don't have to keep My part of the bargain.' It was a two-way covenant, unlike the new covenant which is better. He said to Moses, 'I'll make a nation out of you, Moses—I can leave them, I'm going to.'

'No, You won't, Lord!'

One man stood between the people of God in prevailing prayer. And what happened? He saved the nation. Think of Hannah, ridiculed for drunkenness when in fact she was praying; the little baby that came from her womb turned Israel around. Mother, parent, young person—you can make a difference.

And if you don't stand up and be counted—the Lord will use someone else. You're going to miss it. 'He is no fool who gives what he cannot keep to gain what he cannot lose.'

She said, 'I'll go.' And the rest is history.

Notes

1. Martin Gilbert, *The Holocaust: Record of Destruction*... (Board of Deputies of British Jews, 1978).
2. John Stott, *The Cross of Christ* (IVP, 1986), ch. 13.

3. When Waiting is Progress
(Esther 4:15-7:10)

Watch, now, how God worked it out for the good folks here. Poor Esther is facing huge problems. Her people are about to be annihilated. What on earth is going to happen? What is God going to do? How is He going to work it out for good? In today's chapters we see a lonely girl wondering what to do.

The film *Dead Poets' Society* made a great impact on young people in the Western world. It grossed $94,000,000 at the USA box-office, and in Britain it reached the number one slot in its second week and grossed £6,000,000. Millions saw this film which presents the philosophy of the poet Byron, who taught that to really live life we must *carpe diem*—'seize the day'. In the film an English teacher tries to instil this philosophy in his class of boys. And they set out to do it, to live life to the hilt. One of them tragically dies by suicide, as a result of seizing the day and seizing the opportunity but not having the right balance of experience, and (as I would see it), knowledge of God and His ways and His word. Isn't this desire to 'seize the day' a problem in my life and yours?

Here is Esther, faced with an edict which says her entire people are going to be wiped out in nine months time, and she feels called to do something about it. Just as I felt as a young twenty-two year old at home in Belfast with slaughter all around me: 'Lord, I want to do something about it!' Just as you feel in your town, your home, your college, your street—'Lord I want to do something about the problems

that are around me, and to stand for You.' Esther's prepared
to die for it: 'If I perish, I perish.' So when is the right
moment to go for it? Should she 'seize the day' immediately?
Notice what she does.

She doesn't seize the day. She stands back. 'Go, gather all
the Jews who are present in Shushan, and fast for me: neither
eat nor drink for three days, night or day. My maids and I will
fast likewise. And so I will go to the king, which is against the
law; and if I perish, I perish!' At the very heart of this book
comes a silent interlude. Here is 'waiting for God'. Was it not
the great Amy Carmichael, the first missionary to be sup-
ported by the Keswick Convention, who said: 'Waiting for
God—there's blood and iron in it.' We all love to serve our
Master, we love to be involved in Christian work, to get
excited and be active in it—but oh, to wait for God is so
difficult! But what I want to teach this morning that waiting
can mean winning.

They calm their emotions, get their perspective and stand
back for a little time. It's exactly as Isaiah said: 'Those who
wait on the Lord shall renew their strength; they shall mount
up with wings like eagles, they shall run and not be weary,
they shall walk and not faint' (Isa. 40:31). Are you in that
situation at the moment? You are waiting for God. You don't
want to push or manipulate, to try to worm your way into
something. You are waiting for God to open a door. But
waiting isn't easy, is it? A supermarket queue when the till
breaks down...a motorway traffic jam...a queue at the
bank...But did you ever sit in a fast food restaurant and
listen to the reiterated 'Who's next?...Who's next?...Who's
next?' Everything is rushed and speeded up. It's especially
true of the media. As Os Guinness says in his brilliant book
The Gravedigger File[1]—'Tomorrow the complete scriptures
in a single slogan'; come to church, say a single line, go home.
I know what he's saying. It's hard to wait for things.

Is there a childless couple here this morning waiting for a
child? A single person maybe, waiting for marriage? Somebody chronically sick, watching me somewhere on this video,
listening to this tape, reading this book, waiting for health?
Some dear soul, even, waiting for death? My friend, it's not
easy to wait. Are you emotionally scarred, waiting for peace?

Maybe you're in a dead-end career and you're waiting for a breakthrough. Maybe you're a student, waiting to get on with your life. Maybe you are lonely, longing and waiting to belong to something—believe me, we hope with all our hearts that you feel in these great crowds at Keswick that this is a place where people love you and where you are welcome.

It's hard waiting for God. But wait upon the Lord, and you will renew your strength, you will regain your perspective, you will store up energy and ward off weariness. Do you know the stories of how the eaglet learns to fly? How its mother pushes it out of the nest and then lifts it on her wing, so it learns to fly? I thought that was true for years, until one day an expert in these matters told me, 'It's aerodynamically impossible. By the time it's ready to fly, the eaglet is too big; the mother couldn't hold it. It steps out of the nest and just takes off.' In a spiritual sense I would see that as 'by faith'. So when the Lord says through Moses, in his last great sermon, 'I will bear you, My people, on eagles' wings', if you step out by faith, away you go.

But it's been discovered that the American bald eagle comes in behind its eaglet when it is learning to fly, and with its mighty wings creates air currents that give the young fledgling lift. And the Hebrew word for 'I will bear you on eagle's wings' is 'to lift'. So that when you step out by faith to do something for the Lord—even as I am, in great weakness, ministering to you this morning—my lovely Lord through His Spirit will come near and give you 'lift'! Praise the Lord, He will create the conditions and the atmosphere that the flesh knows nothing of. Oh, that we leaned upon Him more! To be inwardly strengthened by His might; not in the flesh, but in the spirit. Wait upon the Lord, Christian. Is it hard? Oh yes, but look what it will do for you.

And notice how things develop. For three days Esther has waited on the Lord, gained new strength and now it's time to test her wings (5:1-3). Notice, that teaches us that during her time of fasting and waiting God prepared not only her heart, but the hearts of those who opposed her, even those who were unpredictable and hostile. God softened the king's heart towards Esther. She obtained favour in his sight (5:2). He extended the sceptre: 'What do you wish, Queen Esther?

What is your request?' Did she say, 'Execute Haman, give me his head'? No, no, no...she's waiting for God now. She exercises restraint. 'If it pleases the king'—I love verse 4!— 'let the king and Haman come today to the banquet that I have prepared for him.' What self-control—her people are about to be wiped out; wouldn't you have said, 'Oh darling, please, spare my people'? She's married to this man. But she doesn't; she doesn't expand on what's troubling her, she doesn't point a finger at Haman and demand justice. She doesn't manipulate the king. She doesn't fly into a frenzy, she doesn't dissolve into tears, she doesn't act in haste. Instead she issues an invitation to a banquet for that day.

It's worth asking: when would Esther have had time to prepare such a banquet? Even when you don't have to do the nitty-gritty of laying out everything yourself, such banquets take time to prepare. When did she prepare it? During the three days that she was fasting. What does that prove to us as Christians? Waiting on the Lord doesn't mean that you are inactive and inert. Even if you are waiting on God for some breakthrough to come to guide you to future service for Him, that doesn't mean that you and I are to sit back and say, 'Well, there's nothing I can do in the meantime.'

I had a vision in my heart, arising from the concern I mentioned earlier, for a Bible class for all walks of life in Northern Ireland, where no matter where you came from across the divide, you'd feel welcome. It wouldn't have the name of a denomination over it, it wouldn't be a sectarian enterprise, but would simply say: 'We preach Christ crucified; and have you seen the treasure that's in here? It's for you, too.' It was seven-and-a-half years before I saw that come to pass. But that didn't mean I learned that I had to be inactive in the meantime. If God has given you a burden for something and it hasn't come around yet, my friend you can be busy, you can be planning and preparing in the meantime. Esther made full use of the time, and I love that detail.

God does not tell us to wait just to test our patience. He often delays His answer so it'll bring a greater blessing. Esther could have died while she waited; and the plain fact is that many people have waited for God, for something they wanted deeply, and did die in the waiting. Maybe you have a

loved one who had a vision for something which never happened, though they waited for God for so long. Do you know
the story of the young soldier in the American Civil War
whose wounds left him very severely disabled for the rest of
his days, waiting and wrestling with problems, waiting for
God to show His face and His purpose in the terrible dis-
abilities he had received? At the end of his struggles he wrote
the loveliest thing on this subject outside of the Bible that
I've ever read. Many of you know it.

> I asked for strength that I might achieve, and I was made weak
> that I might obey. I asked for health that I might do greater
> things; I was given infirmity that I might do better things. I asked
> for riches that I might be happy; I was given poverty that I might
> be wise. I asked for power that I might have the praise of men; I
> was given weakness that I might feel the need of God. I asked for
> all things that I might enjoy life; I was given life that I might
> enjoy all things. I have received nothing I asked for and all that I
> hoped for. My prayer is answered.

Sarah laughed the laugh of a cynic as she waited for God.
And Abraham laughed the laugh of faith. You're allowed a
spiritual chuckle now and again. 'Just you wait and see what
my God can do!' How many of you here this morning were
like I was when I started out in my ministry—thoroughly
discouraged? I met a Christian one day in a certain town
square in Ireland, 'Oh Derick,' he said, 'I hear you've given
up teaching to go into Christian work.' He added, 'Of course,
if it doesn't work out you can always go back to teaching'! I
do have a spiritual chuckle now and again. If God wants me
back in teaching I'll go tomorrow, but you know the simple
fact is, as I said to a dear Japanese brother here last night—a
young man of God seeking to serve Him—'If God, my dear
brother, calls you to something, He will never make a fool
out of you.'

You may be a fool for Christ's sake in the eyes of the
world, but I have found, as you have found, that God will
never cause us to blush because of His word. Don't be
ashamed. It'll stand anywhere. Before a heinous king like
Ahasuerus, or in your quiet country home perhaps, or in
some little village where you work for God. Don't bargain

with Him—'Lord, I'll wait for You and if You show me what to do, then, if You heal my child...', 'Lord, give me a husband but let it be Jimmy', 'Lord I want a wife but let it be Mary', or whatever. If you don't bargain with God you'll get abundantly more than you could ever ask or think. Young person, have you ever picked that up? It's not our motivation for doing it, but that's what happens. We do it for His glory.

Now in 5:9-14, the spotlight suddenly falls on Haman, the man who's behind the plan to exterminate all the Jews. Look at his priorities, how much money he had, how many sons he had in that passage—what a high position! Notice that he was a person who was self-absorbed. He wanted everybody to bow down to him and he absolutely hated the one man who just wouldn't do it.

His wife (verse 14) came up with a solution that would keep Mordecai from spoiling her husband's dinner with the king. 'Have a gallows built, 75 feet high, in the morning, and ask the king to hang him on it: and then go to the dinner with the king and be happy.' What kind of a wife was that? He took her advice and had the gallows built.

Here is Haman. He thinks he's got everything, doesn't he? But isn't it interesting in 5:11-13 that although he has all his ambitions, he's still disappointed? There's still something preying on his soul. It's a paradox, isn't it? That the people of God are frequently sorrowful but they can always rejoice, yet the world, when it gets what it wants, is still dissatisfied.

> Now none but Christ can satisfy
> None other name for me
> There's love and life and lasting joy
> Lord Jesus, found in thee.

None but Christ can satisfy; but the world—why it's a bucket with a hole in it, we're never satisfied. 'For a little while, if need be, you have been grieved by various trials...yet believing, you rejoice with joy inexpressible and full of glory' (1 Pet. 1:6,8). Why do we endure? Because we see One who is invisible. It's like that reference to Moses 'choosing rather to suffer affliction with the people of God than to enjoy the passing pleasures, esteeming the reproach of Christ greater riches than the treasures in Egypt' (Heb. 11:25-26).

The raising of Mordecai to prominence is one of the most amazing examples in all history of the simple truth that when all seems lost, it isn't. The gallows are erected. Mordecai's to be hung. Haman's got the edict to wipe the people of God out. Everything seems lost. Is that how you are this morning? Oh Christian, a simple word to your heart and mine in the Lord's presence: when all seems lost, it isn't.

Mordecai hadn't been promoted even though he had stopped an assassination of the king. And that seemed very hard. He hadn't been rewarded at the time of his kind act, and this wicked fellow was; and now and the gallows waits for Mordecai. And I want to ask, what miracle will happen now to save him? Will thunder fall? Will the earth open up and swallow them? Will angels carry Mordecai away? Will a chariot of fire call at the king's gate and take him home to be with the Lord? Will he be hidden from his pursuers? No. God will save him by His providence. Mordecai will have both life and glory without a miracle. Tell me, will it be a friend that God will send to the king to remind him that he owes Mordecai his life because of what he did earlier to save him from assassination? Will there be a petition from the Jews? A local press campaign? Where in all the world will you find someone who, within twenty-four hours, will save this man of God from execution? Who will remind the king of his obligation to exalt, not hang, this man?

Are you a modern Mordecai? Have you been overlooked? Then learn from the story. Are you in some obscure place— you love the Lord and you long for some kind of recognition from God, or blessing in the salvation of souls, or some evidence that the Lord is still with you? Let me remind you of the words of Scripture this morning. 'God is not unjust to forget your work and labour of love which you have shown towards his name' (Heb. 6:10). 'Your heavenly Father who has seen in secret will reward you openly' (Matt. 6). No work done for God is insignificant. Jesus noticed the widow's mite. So what will God do? Where will deliverance come for these people?

It will come from something as insignificant as insomnia.

The king can't sleep (6:1). Does he call for musicians? No. He calls for a historian. Who would read history in the middle of the night to get to sleep? And the account was read of Mordecai, who had saved Ahasuerus from assassination. 'What!' he says. 'Has this man been honoured?' No—he's been forgotten. Then the king asked, 'Who is in the court?' And Haman was just coming into the outer court to suggest (6:4) that the king hang Mordecai on the gallows that he had prepared. They told him Haman was there.

'Bring him in,' he said. 'Excuse me Haman'—if I can paraphrase it—'what would you do for the man that the king delights to honour?' And Haman said, 'Wow, it must be me, there's nobody in all the world like me. Let's go mad.' And his mind goes crazy. 'Give him a royal robe and a horse on which the king has ridden and a royal crest on his head and let this robe and horse be delivered to the hand of one of the king's most noble princes that he may array the man whom the king delights to honour, parade him on horseback through the city square'—take a breath, think of something more, oh yes!—'Thus shall it be done to the man whom the king delights to honour!'

'OK,' said the king, 'do it for Mordecai the Jew.'

Wow! What a moment. And where did it all come from? From an old, wicked, miserable king who couldn't sleep.

Do you think it'll come to you through some great invitation through the letterbox one day? From some mighty person who has a string of degrees the length of your arm, or from a contact in some favoured circle? No! When will we stop leaning upon self and lean on our God?

How powerful the song which Paul Sandberg sang to us at the beginning of our meeting this morning! I had heard already about how ill he had been. You know, he didn't think he would have to go through tests and have a kidney transplant. Do you know what he said to me this week? He said, 'Derick, it's as if I've been taken off the shelf and used again.' He never dreamed he'd sing in a place like this. But God had a plan for him.

And I want to tell Paul, 'You've seen nothing yet.' Because he's going to sing in front of a multitude that no computer could compute, or that could be captured on video or tape, because there'll be such a crowd you could never get the camera or microphone to cover the whole lot. Heaven. What a lovely song! It didn't work out the way you thought it would.

What are we trying to say this morning? We're trying to say, 'There is nothing fortuitous; nothing happens without God.' Would you think of ascribing to God something as seemingly unimportant a matter as insomnia? But the insomnia is an essential link in the chain of events. It's the king-pin! Take that away and the rest of this story is useless. Another night's sleep, and Mordecai would have been in his grave. There is nothing casual to God, even a restless night for a human creature. In Him we live and move and have our being.

Stephen Hawking, the atheistic professor of mathematics at Cambridge, says 'There is no such a thing as creation. There is no such a thing as a personal God. The law of physics is that which runs the world.' No! The Bible tells us that our God feeds ravens and sees little sparrows fall. And I know of no more beautiful truth than that which you can take away from here, saying in your heart: 'All things work together for good to them that love God.' Wait for God, Christian. It may simply be somebody who can't sleep at night who will change your day.

Note

1. Os Guinness, *The Gravedigger File* (Hodder and Stoughton, 1983), p. 171.

4. When God Moves the Immovable
(Esther 8:1-10:3)

What we are looking at today is a God who can move the immovable. There is no scene so dark that God cannot brighten it, no writing so permanent that He cannot change it, no heart so hard that He cannot soften it even if that hard heart resides in the most powerful person on earth. Here is the king of a vast empire, a despot whose word is law: he has absolute power over his people. And through Haman the Jew-hater he has overseen a plan devised to exterminate all the Jews in his empire and ratified it in an edict which could not be changed. Daniel 5 and 6 speak of the unalterable law of the Medes and the Persians. The whole thing looks absolutely impossible. Can God, in this situation, move the immovable? And the answer is yes: He can.

We've got to understand that our God can break through the impossible. Are you trying to tell me this morning that it is impossible for God to change your circumstances? Even on this final morning together, after the lovely week we've had, in the presence of God together both morning and evening, as our brethren have ministered together to you from this pulpit—are you really saying, at the end of all that you have heard, 'It's not going to change when I go home in my situation, my circumstances will never change'?

You may have troubles pursuing you wherever you turn. You know, impossibilities can either drive us to God or devour us, leaving the carcass for the scavengers of depres-

sion and inferiority and loneliness to pick apart. But no
problem that enters your life can come in for the kill unless
you let it. Your hope will die if you keep focusing on the
impossibilities, and the more obsessed you become with them
the more it will squeeze the very life out of you. And you'll
give up, saying, 'He...she...they...will never change: it's
impossible.'

I've reminded you this week of the mocking Sarah. She
laughed in mockery at the Lord's promise to give her a child.
'It's impossible' she said. And the Lord said to Abraham,
'Why did Sarah laugh? Is there anything too hard for the
Lord?' Do you remember that statement of Jeremiah: 'Ah,
Lord God! Behold, you have made the heavens and the earth
by your great power and outstretched arm. There is nothing
too hard for you' (Jer. 32:17)? Have you heard that, my
brother, my sister, wherever you are listening, watching or
reading—on tape, video or printed page across the world;
perhaps you are not a Christian, but you're watching or
listening: we say to you from the word of God, 'Is there
anything too hard for the Lord?' We're not gathered around
a sect or denomination this morning. We are gathered all one
in Christ Jesus. And it's not just theology and teaching we're
into. We are worshipping, and living for, a living God.

'Then the word of the Lord came to Jeremiah, saying,
"Behold I am the Lord, the God of all flesh. Is there anything
too hard for me?" ' (Jer. 32:27). Let me be very practical in
this final Bible reading. Substitute your own problem. 'Is
your marriage too hard for Me?'; 'Is your local church too
hard for Me?'; 'Is your business too hard for Me?'; 'Is your
health too hard for Me?'; 'Is your alcoholism too hard for
me?'; 'Is your drug addiction too hard for Me?'; 'Is your
smoking too hard for Me?'; 'Are your sins too hard for Me?'

Now don't misunderstand me and fall out with me on the
last morning, please! But can I suggest something to you?
The historian was brought in to the king when he had insomnia, reading things to him that had happened. Now, what
does that verse mean, 'Your sins and your iniquities I will
remember no more' (Heb. 8, 10)? Many people have problems with that verse. Does it mean that God forgets that I
have sinned, the things that I did? Don't think me sarcastic:

but do you think that God the Father in heaven looks across at Christ the Son and sees the nail-prints of Calvary in His hands, and says 'I cannot for the life of Me remember how those nail-prints got there, or what caused them?'

It seems to me, when you link this verse up with the rest of Scripture, that Scripture is teaching us categorically that the penal law that stood against us for our sins—the legal justice of God that should have fallen upon my sinful, Christless head—can no longer touch me. The blood of Jesus Christ His son cleanses us from one or two sins? All sins! You say, 'What about that skeleton in the cupboard?' That one too, friends. It means that no historian will stand in heaven, bring out his book and read, 'Derick Bingham did this and that and the other.' No. In that sense there will be no remembrance of my sins. They won't be called up against me because they are forgiven and cleansed. I am free. It is not that God forgets what I did; it's that he refuses to bring it up against me. It's gone. Brother and sister, if that doesn't thrill your heart, I don't know what will. That's the great message at the very heart of the gospel: forgiveness and cleansing in Christ. So your sins are not too hard for Him. Are your temptations too hard for Him? The things, said Christ, which are impossible with men are possible with God.

So you're at the end of your rope? You say 'I've tried everything'? Well, what is God saying? Is He saying 'All things are possible to him who worries'? A friend used to say to me, 'Why pray when you can worry?' Some Christians, I find, if they're really enjoying the word and enjoying the Lord are saying to themselves, 'There must be something wrong—I'm enjoying it.'

'All things are possible to him who worries?' No. 'All things are possible to him who attempts to work it out for himself, or by himself?' No. All things are possible to him who believes, and without faith it is impossible to please God.

We see now how Esther, having fasted with her friends, now begins to move in and strike at the very heart of the king. In 8:1-4 the king's heart changes from one that gave the Jews into Haman's hands to one who gave Haman's estate into the hands of two Jews. The king (verse 2) gave his signet ring, which he had taken from Haman, to Mordecai; and Esther appointed Mordecai over the house of Haman. And then in verse 3 she implores the king to counteract the evil plot of Haman against the Jews. Can God move the immovable? Yes. That wicked heart is transformed. 'Certainly, Esther. The first edict cannot be revoked, but you can issue a second in my name to counteract it.'

Again, I want to be practical, Christian. I want to encourage you. God can move impossible hearts. My friend Duncan Donaldson was imprisoned eighty times for drunkenness. He used to steal the sweet counter in Woolworth's at a single swipe. When he was drunk six policemen couldn't control him. He used to roll home every night drunk and kick the front door in. He got saved listening to the preaching of the word one evening, and that night he came home quiet and converted, opened his front door and his own dog bit him! Why? Because it thought he was a stranger.

You'll be a better grocer, a better doctor, a better teacher if you know Christ. Your children will see the difference, your boss will see the difference, the matron in your hospital where you work will see the difference, the neighbours will see the difference, even your dog will see the difference. Our Lord Jesus changes everything! Praise God! We are new creatures in Christ Jesus. Duncan went on Scottish television one night. 'No preaching in this interview,' they said. Duncan didn't preach, he just wore a T-shirt across his huge barrel chest and the T-shirt said on it 'Under new management'. The whole of Scotland got the message. He used to sit in church meetings with that on his chest. It wasn't the average Keswick-type T-shirt, but I tell you I could hardly preach for the sermon coming from Duncan's T-shirt. God moves!

I want to be practical, to speak into the most practical area of your life. Are you going home to a drunken husband? Maybe teenagers who have no interest whatsoever in our Bible teaching this week, who are way out there in the world? Impossible hearts, like Ahasuerus' heart as God moved it and changed it.

God can move an immovable edict, as you see in 8:9-14. The king's heart had softened; Haman had been put to death;

now Esther had to confront the difficult problem of the royal edict. I want to repeat, the first edict was not annulled, though the second did so in effect by giving the Jews the right not only to defend themselves but to take severe retaliatory action. This counter-measure put fear into the enemies of the Jews and averted genocide. It was a turning-point for them.

Now God begins to penetrate the impenetrable gloom. Haman's dead, this shadow and menace of the edict are lifted; the people had been living in a death-row atmosphere, a people marked for destruction—until they received that second edict, which gave them the authority to use self-defence.

I don't want to allegorise too far this morning, but—thank God for the new covenant. Under the old one, if you were caught gathering sticks on the Sabbath you were dead. Under the new covenant, 'once in Christ in Christ for ever thus, the eternal covenant stands'. Peter sinned and denied his Lord, but he found that neither his sin, his temperament nor his denial had changed the Lord's commitment to him. The biggest shock in Peter's life, when he saw the Master making them their breakfast by the lake-side, was this: 'He still loves me.'

George Matheson, at a time of great disappointment, when his heart was almost broken, his faith in shreds and his sight gone, wrote that lovely hymn, 'Oh love that will not let me go, I rest my weary soul in Thee.' It's powerful truth, isn't it? And I think of that lovely verse, 'The law of the Spirit of life in Christ Jesus has set me free from the law of sin and death' (Rom. 8:2). Brother, sister, can I put this to you gently this morning? What do you owe the flesh? What did it ever do for you? Pride, envy and all that—what did it ever do for you?

Paul in Romans teaches that we're now rooted in the Spirit. You're not rooted in the flesh any more. You've got new roots, you're growing in new ground: resurrection, redemption ground, a new creature in Christ Jesus. Just as the Lord will transform this earth and redeem it, so He's started that process in you and me. So why give any allegiance to the flesh and the devil and the world? Why pander to him and play to him and go into that yoke of bondage again? Oh Christian, what ails you? Are you away after the flesh again? Am I? When we know it will never do anything for us, and never has done? Let's sow to the spirit in this coming year and months, and not to the flesh. As we're rooted in the spirit now, we're set free from the law of sin and death.

Esther 9 brings us to a difficult section. I want to get to the heart of it, I don't want to run past it. We see now God controlling the people's irresistible temptation.

Mark Twain said, 'Everyone is like the moon and has a dark side which they never show to anybody.' The vast majority of us have a problem. We react too quickly to things. Remember Naomi telling Ruth not to rush matters. 'Be still my soul, the Lord is on thy side.' But you and I react far too quickly don't we? We've all been in situations where we have talked too much and later regretted it.

In Esther's story a problem raises its head which all of us have trouble controlling: that of retaliation. The Jews had been granted the right not only to self-defence, but to retaliation and plunder. That's a pretty powerful thing to be granted. Mordecai's counter-decree had gone out on 25 June 474 BC, so the Jews had most of that summer and autumn as well as the winter months to prepare for 7 March 473 BC, which was the day the original edict would have matured and genocide taken place. But on the day when the enemies of the Jews hoped to gain the mastery over them, it was turned to the contrary so that the Jews themselves gained the mastery over those who had hated them. It was a great and memorable day.

But notice 9:5—'Thus the Jews defeated all their enemies with the stroke of the sword, with slaughter and destruction, and did what they pleased with those who hated them.' What does that tell me? It suggests that on that day some of the Jews did not confine themselves to self-defence, because the best defence is sometimes a tactical offence—and there is no question that God had chosen Israel occasionally as a destructive instrument against those who reject the true God. But the wording of this verse has proved to be highly offensive to many, and it must be understood in its context.

Some people, too, find Esther's request for the hanging of Haman's sons and the public display of their corpses vengeful (9:6-10, 13-14). If the enemies of the Jews had been decisively defeated and were now willing to leave the Jews in peace, then Esther's request certainly would have been vengeful. If, however, there still remained in Susa pockets of resistance intending a second round with the Jews, then Esther's request would be realistic and necessary, and the exposure and desecration of Haman's sons could be understood as a deterrent.

Esther's request in 9:15 for the decree to be extended one more day to permit the Jews to kill their enemies is also seen as very vindictive. Yet though Scripture doesn't specifically say so, it seems valid to assume that Queen Esther had learned of another Persian plot to attack the Jews of Susa on the following day as well. And therefore she asked permission for the Jews to defend themselves on a second day again, and the king allowed it. If revenge was the primary reason for the second day's fighting, the author doesn't give any hint of it. He does not glory in the details of the battle concerning the fighting itself, he just states the time and the place and the casualty figures.

The Jews slew 75,000 people, which seems a lot. Yet when you consider the vast extent of the Persian empire it is understandable; it is actually very few in comparison to what had been planned for them. In the light of the difficulty of chapter 9 and the Jewish nation of that time, the remarkable thing that the Holy Spirit seems to emphasise is the restraint that was in fact exercised. The Jews were legally sanctioned to utterly destroy their enemies, down to women and children (8:11). They could kill whoever they liked, even pillage and plunder their enemies. But nowhere in 9:1-16 are women and children mentioned as killed. And (9:10,15,16)—'they did not lay their hands on the plunder.'

The temptation to go too far must have been great. But they pulled in their reins. They didn't run through the streets in wild, unrestrained violence. And I think the Holy Spirit is emphasising this in this passage specifically. Self-control is a wonderful quality in a person's life. The temptation to go too

far faces everybody. The limit on your credit card, the tempt-
ing buffet lunch—and in the moral realm, too, we all have a
problem. 'For the good that I will to do, I do not do,' said
Paul. 'But the evil I will not to do, that I practise' (Rom.
7:19). We all have that temptation to go too far. But the key
to holding back is self-control, of attitude, feelings, actions.
Maybe you're discouraged in that area this morning. Well I'm
glad to be able to tell you that love is that which the Holy
Spirit, God's love, sheds abroad in your heart. I tell you,
Christian, self-control is one of the gifts of the Spirit (cf. Gal.
5:22-23). That will get you out of all that slavery. When
you're tempted to take matters into your own hands, to strike
back, to get even—may you be filled with the Holy Spirit.
How we need this in Northern Ireland in these days! 'How do
you do it?' you say. 'Be practical. How *can* we have self-
control?' Well, I really do think it has to do with the mind. 'It
is not what you think you are, it is what you think—you are.'
As a man thinks in his own heart, so is he.

How can I, standing against all the worldly fleshly things
that bombard me every day, have self-control? We all need
it, I need it as much as you do. How am I not going to be
conformed to this world but transformed? The answer, says
Scripture, is by the renewing of my mind. It begins in the
mind. And if that mind is controlled and every thought
brought into captivity by the Spirit, you will be controlled in
your minds at the centre and the circumference will take care
of itself. May the Holy Spirit help us in that area as we lean
upon His power, so there will be restraint.

Charles Swindoll, in his study guide on Esther, brings in
this point very powerfully. He says that it is often easier for us
to enter into eulogies at a funeral than excitement at a wed-
ding. In Ireland people sometimes ask, 'Was it a good
funeral? Did you meet so-and-so? Did you talk with them?'
Isn't it strange? Suffering the aches and pains of life, and
celebrating the happy times, are two different things.

You may say, 'Well, we're not like the Irish.' Are you not?
How often have you said to a friend, 'I've got a pain in my
leg,' and they say, 'I know a cousin of mine who had that and
they had their leg removed.' You're in the kitchen and the
spin drier is making an ugly noise and your Great-Aunt

Emma says 'I read in the paper the other day somebody's spin drier caught fire and it burned their house down.' You have a misery story and there's always going to be somebody who'll top it with a much more dramatic one. Is life meant to be a misery to be endured? No! But a lot of people live like that.

I studied the Danish philosopher Søren Kierkegaard at university. He once said, 'Life can only be understood backwards—but it must be lived forwards.' There's a straight line in life, as I've been saying to you each morning. 'I can see a straight line to this point, but what happens from here on, I don't know'—well, in a sense that's true; but have you ever thought why we tend to be more comfortable with lamentation than we are with celebration? A lot of it has to do with the fact that we focus wistfully on the past. If ninety people out of this crowd come to me and say, 'Thank you, Derick, for that message,' and one person says, 'You're a liberal, you use the wrong translation, I hate your stories—can't stand the sight of you anyway, hope they never have you back'— who do I remember? You remember the insensitive rather than the inspirational. This is a real problem in our lives. I have it and you have it, and it's a problem that we're going to have to overcome. As we look back at events and circumstances we tend to analyse and remember catastrophes rather than celebrations. Weddings, births, happy Christmasses past, good holidays, joyful times—they blur at the edges.

The Northern Ireland that I have lived in for the last twenty years of my ministry is an Ulster full of tragedy, sorrow, divorce and moral breakdown. I can easily find my memories being overwhelmed by the negative and forget what God has done. Like Joshua, when he came up the Jordan against Ai and lay down and moaned (cf. Josh. 7,8). God had to tell him to get up; he'd forgotten about crossing the Red Sea and the past blessings and so on. We so easily forget the blessings of God. God has brought you all this way, Christian, and He's not going to desert you.

Maybe you've made a wrong decision in the past and you feel you are going to be God's second-best for the rest of your life. Jim Packer has said that some people regard the will of God as being like a holiday itinerary on holiday: if you're at

that hospital and at that bus-stop and at that airport at the
right time that's fine, but if you miss one of them then you're
second-best in the rest. But God's will is not like a holiday
itinerary. Maybe you genuinely misread what God wanted
earlier in your life—does that mean that you're God's second-best until the day you die? Christian, if you believe that,
that's downright unbelief. Are you trying to tell me that the
God who can move an impossible edict, and break an impossible heart down, and come powerfully into this impenetrable
gloom, and hold these people back from an irresistible temptation to go on the rampage—do you think that the God who
can do that can't reverse that mistake or misunderstanding,
and use you again?

Of course He can! What kind of a God do you think you
have? 'Oh, Mary is second-best'... 'Tom is second-best'. No,
you're not second best! The Lord can forgive and restore you
and use you again. 'One thing I do,' says Paul, 'forgetting
those things which are behind and reaching forward to those
things which are ahead, I press towards the goal for the prize
of the upward call of God in Christ Jesus' (Phi. 3:13).

So they introduce this feast of Purim. The word *pur* is an
ancient word for a die, a lot that's cast. Haman cast that die
to determine what day would be best for the Jews' destruction. But what appeared to be a day of extermination turned
into a day of celebration. They named that day, set apart for
the feast of Purim, after the very thing that had first sounded
their death knell—the dice that he threw.

In Alabama, the cotton crop on which the town's economy
depended was once destroyed by boll weevils. The farmers
struck back by planting peanuts, which boll weevils detest.
Soon the plague was over and the economy recovered. The
townspeople erected a monument in the town to the boll
weevil that had destroyed their crops. It's the same spirit.
They turned a symbol of defeat into a symbol of victory.

To this very day Jews celebrate the Feast of Purim. A
synagogue guide described it to me: 'The rabbi reads the
Book of Esther, and every time Haman's name is mentioned
the kids are allowed to boo, and every time Esther or Mordecai is mentioned we're allowed to shout Hooray!' The
children go hunting for little pastry Hamans and Mordecais

that their fathers have hidden, and the rabbi even throws sweets to the children—in the synagogue!

It's a celebration, you see. Wonderful! And I hope that we too will understand what great things God has done for us in the past, and raise a mental memorial in our minds. Maurice Rowlandson, so long the Secretary of this Convention, once showed me his system of five-by-three cards. He writes down on them one blessing that has happened every day of his life. A doctor who is a church elder once told me, when I said was becoming depressed in my work, 'Keep a diary, Derick. And when the Lord blesses you or somebody says it was a good message, write it down.' Do you know, a Baptist pastor I knew in Ireland once approached Martin Lloyd-Jones and said, 'Thank you for that message'; he replied, 'Thank you, brother. Very few people say that to me.' What, that great giant of a man? The people you think are being encouraged the most are sometimes being encouraged the least.

So remember the past.

The Book of Esther stands on history's shelf like a condensed version of life itself. The fate of God's people was hanging in the balance. In the end God triumphed over impending tragedy. And He will do that for us. They won, and we will win. 'And God will wipe away every tear from their eyes' (Rev. 7:17, cf. Isa. 65:19). And there will be no more death nor sorrow nor crying and there shall be no more pain, for the former things have passed away. What a day, Christian, we're headed for! We have the sovereign assurance from the word of God that there will be a happy ending to the story.

What overcomes the world? What is the victory? Our faith. The story of Esther ends with the same king, the same kingdom, the same country, the same realm of authority, the same manner of ruling—but unlike the beginning of the story there's been a major change; Mordecai has replaced Haman. What a lovely vision that man had. If he had just stuck in his own street and said, 'What can I do about it?' what would have happened?—if he'd just said, 'I can't do anything about it, I'm staying here'? Just a guy who sat at the king's gate...

What are the final lessons of the Book of Esther?

When God wins, the people He uses are often unexpected ones. The gate-keeper became the mighty man in the nation. God used an unlikely person. I was given yesterday a history of all the speakers at the Keswick convention. I've been reading them through the night. Hudson Taylor. Dwight L. Moody. F. B. Meyer. W. P. Nicholson. Harry Ironside. Bishop Handley Moule. And on it goes...

And I felt like weeping. All those characters, the saints of God of the past! Hudson Taylor's girlfriend gave him up because she didn't want to go to China—yet he went. Think of the heartache of all those men of God. None of us is a whole, independent, self-sufficient, super-capable, all-powerful hot-shot. Let's quit acting like we are. Our God can use you and can use me, if we are available. The message is a big one. It says in the very last verse of the Book of Esther that Mordecai had sought 'the good of his people and speaking peace to all his kindred'. When God wins, the message He honours most often is universal. The whole empire was touched.

Through the doubts, storms, heartaches and trials of your life and mine, let's make this morning service a great altar. Let's all lay our lives on the altar. Then, I dare to believe, the four corners of the earth can be touched as a result of this two weeks together at Keswick this year; because when God wins, the message He honours most is universal. The people who have vision, who look beyond themselves and look out for others... that's the kind of vision and the kind of people that God uses. So come away just from your own front door, your own home, your own village, your own city, your own street—let's go away home with a world vision—'not my interests, but the Lord's interests'. Of course, that's the very heart of the gospel, isn't it: Esther and Mordecai were expendable. They laid their lives, the pair of them, down, on the altar, said 'If I perish I perish'—and look at the result.

So Christian, what does the Book of Esther say? It says, categorically, do what is right and leave the rest with God. It says, ultimately, that our God reigns. You have come to the kingdom for a time such as this; don't miss your opportunity.

'The Saving Message of the Cross' (1 Corinthians 1:18)

by Dr Raymond Brown

1. The Searching Judge (Matthew 26:1–27:66)

The four accounts of the story of the cross in the Gospels have been identified by New Testament scholars as the 'Passion narratives', and there's no reason to quarrel in any way with that description, which conveys the suffering of the Lord Jesus and the events which led up immediately to it.

The importance of the Gospel writers

I believe that there are different portraits of Christ given in these chapters. Matthew wanted to communicate to his contemporary readers, the first readers of his Gospel, that although the Lord Jesus was being judged by others in a trial—and a mock trial at that—what is clearly and unmistakably happening in this situation is that men and women are being judged. Jesus is the searching judge in Matthew's Passion narrative, exposing the sin of the men and women who surrounded Him. Some surrounding Him were His closest friends and forsook Him. Some were bitter enemies, ruthless in their determination to execute Him. And some were strangers, but through these events came to know Him deeply.

Three things are of the greatest importance when we come to give ourselves to the all-important exercise of understanding the message of Scripture. First we must seek by the best means that we can, and supremely under the inspiration of God's Holy Spirit, to understand what the particular passage before us may have meant to its first readers. What was it saying to the Christians of the first century?

Secondly we must ask, what is it saying to a twentieth-century reading public? In other words, because it is God's word it is not saying something which is locked away in the past. It has a message which is strikingly relevant to us. What is this passage, written in the first century, saying to us about life in the late twentieth century?

But there is a third question we must ask. What is it saying to *me*? In other words, we can discern clearly what it may be saying to first-century readers. We can see that it has power-ful and persuasive application in the late twentieth century. But we can go away from it unchanged. What is it saying to me? It's important that we ask that about these Passion narratives.

I've called this series 'The saving message of the cross', recalling the words of the apostle Paul to that troublesome and fractious church at Corinth in the first century—that the saving message of the cross is essential for those of us 'who are being saved' (1 Cor. 1:18). Not just '*were* saved', but who *are*, as a daily process, *being* saved. These are three great dimensions of our faith. It was a glorious moment of course when we came to appreciate that Christ's death was for us, whether or not we can point to the date of that realisation on a calendar. Yet it's so important for us to understand we *were* saved, but are also *being* saved day-by-day and *will be* saved. It's that ongoing process of salvation that will surely benefit us and we will be enriched, challenged and fortified by what we read in this marvellous book; every single part of it is vital for our Christian lives. And surely we as committed evangel-icals stand by the centrality of what distinguished Congrega-tional theologian P. T. Forsyth called the 'cruciality of the cross'. Without the saving message of this cross, we cannot be brought to the place of forgiveness and life-transforming power in our own experience. So these passages are surely vital.

I want daringly to suggest to you that though we as evan-gelicals are committed to that truth, and find ourselves time and again in our experience gathering with gratitude at that cross, there is a very grave and serious danger. We may pay lip-service to that truth, but is it always so central? I love modern hymns and songs; so please do not think for a moment I am tilting at them. I am not. But a few years ago I looked through a book of modern Christian songs, most of which have been an inspiration to me; I found myself rather sobered by the fact that so few of them had direct reference to the cross of Christ. They dealt with a whole range of true, important themes which I do not belittle. But most of them did not take me to the place where Jesus died for me.

I wonder too whether, because we love the story of the cross, we presume that we know these Passion narratives really well. But do we? I want to suggest to you in these Bible Readings that the gifted writers of these beautiful narratives, inspired by God's gracious Spirit, not only brought to their task their own personality, sensitivity, and spiritual awareness prompted by God's Spirit; they had particular needs of the audience in mind while they wrote. Each records features that the other three do not mention. They have different perspectives and are saying important things. That their message is important cannot be denied.

At least a third of Matthew and Mark, a good quarter of Luke and quite half of John deal with the events, sayings and teaching of Jesus in the last week of His life. If you were to read a modern biography and half-way through you found you were reading about the last week of that person's life, you would be astonished. But such is the centrality and cruciality of the cross that the writers of these Gospels give a major amount of space to it. They know that that is why Christ came into the world; not just to live among us, but to die for us and be raised from the dead by God's own power.

The detail of the Gospel writers

The detail in these narratives is astonishing!

The sounds that come to us through them if we read them carefully and sensitively—and meditate (which I'm sure is rather a lost art among evangelicals) on the message of Scripture; not reading it hurriedly, assuming that we know it already or eagerly grasping some thought that we never understood before, and then moving on quickly to something else—but just waiting before it and lingering to hear the sounds. The jingling of silver coins. The pouring of wine at a supper table. The pouring of water into a basin. The governor's wife whispering in his ear. The clashing of swords and clubs, the hammering of nails, the crowing of a cock repeatedly in the early morning.

And the people who are involved; some named—Pilate, Herod, Judas, Barabbas, Peter, John, the mother of Jesus—some unnamed; priests, scribes, soldiers, disciples, women and crowds and thieves.

And the people who are caught up unwillingly in the events; a youth who follows Jesus, scantily dressed, probably roused from his bed by what he's heard; and then suddenly feeling a soldier's hand placed heavily on his garment, realising his life is in danger hurries away leaving his robe in the hands of the soldiers, and flees naked through the streets back home to shelter and safety.

A man on a journey going into the city, not having anything to do with it all; but suddenly he is seized and made to carry the *patibulum*, even though he doesn't know the offender; not because the offender has collapsed (there is nothing in at all in the Gospels to suggest that Jesus fell on His journey to the cross) but because that moment was part of God's design; he is going to carry the cross behind Jesus, as millions and millions after him are to do through the centuries.

A thief, who felt the extreme pain as Jesus did, as the nails were driven through his hands and his feet. He began, like the other thief, to curse Him. He wanted to put the blame on somebody. But as he hung in pain and anguish he came to see the greatest truth that any man or woman could ever see in their lives; that Jesus is all He claims to be. 'Lord, while they're mocking You as king, I want You to know that You are the king. Remember me when you come to Your kingdom.'

A soldier standing at the cross. Wishing above all else, as the minutes ticked by, that he'd never driven those nails into those beautiful hands. And as he sees how Jesus dies he says, 'Surely He was all that they said He wasn't. He was the Son of God.'

Oh my friends, what a story it is! God forgive us if at any moment in our lives through our preoccupation, business or ambition—even our service, even the busy-ness of life—if, for whatever reason, we forget the wonder, shame, mystery and majesty of it. Christ died for us! The just for the unjust, that He might bring us to God.

It's not only the detail and the people and the sounds and the events and the people uninvolved or drawn into it. There is such poignancy in the unforgettable sayings around the cross.

The saying of irritated complaint, even from those who really loved Jesus—'Why the appalling waste of this ointment, so precious, when so many people might have benefited?'

The saying of soul-searching introspection—'Surely not I, Lord!'.

The cry of painful anguish—'Father if it is possible let this cup pass from Me.'

The words of appalling deceit. A man comes through the crowd to kiss Jesus, and, as Matthew records, kisses Him passionately—'Greetings, Rabbi'.

The words of callous indifference from the priests as that man goes back to those priests clutching the money in his hands, wishing he'd never touched it. 'I have sinned!' They say, 'What's that to us? That's your responsibility.'

The words of penitent faith—'Lord, remember me'. The words of unashamed allegiance—'This was the Son of God'.

What detail in these matchless, priceless stories! And I believe that through all eternity, though we shall sing with gratitude and infectious joy and exuberance of all that the Lord has been to us through our lives, it will be time and again that we shall glory in that cross, that Christ died for us and rose again.

What is important in these narratives is not just their importance, their detail, their individuality. Let me ask you, to see how well you really do know the story of the cross, four questions.

Do you know which writer of a Gospel tells you that Judas returned the money? Only one does.

Do you know which writer tells you the incident about the young man whose robe was snatched, so that he hurried home unclothed? Only one does.

Do you know the Gospel where a group of women, as their custom doubtless was in the first century, sought to seek to help and bring comfort—perhaps even practical help—to the criminals who were on their way to be crucified? Only one Gospel writer tells us about the women whom Jesus spoke to on His way to His cross. Do you remember which?

Only one Gospel writer tells us that even in His last moments Jesus was concerned about practical things such as who would look after His dear mother.

Did you pass the test? It was Matthew, Mark, Luke and John in that order.

The detail is important. They didn't just hurriedly write things down. Writing was quite a laborious process in the first century. It's easy for us with our ball-point pens and smooth paper. We can write quickly and effectively. You couldn't do that in the first century. Writing was a very difficult business and quite costly. Therefore you thought about your words. You only said what you really wanted to say.

So it is important that we look at this marvellous story told by four writers in great detail.

The purpose of the Gospel writers

What was their purpose? Well their primary purpose of course was to explain why Jesus died. But I want to suggest to you that their secondary purpose is also of great importance to us. They not only wrote to explain why Jesus died, but to teach how Christians are meant to live.

The three great writers of New Testament letters each remind us of the importance of the death of Christ—not only that we might be saved, but that we might live at our best as Christians. The apostle Paul: 'And he died for all, that those who live should no longer live to themselves but for him who died for them and was raised again' (2 Cor. 5:15). In other words, He died to deliver us from our self-centredness and our preoccupation. Peter: He died 'leaving you an example' (1 Pet. 2:21)—the word translated 'example' is the word that you would use in first-century education to describe the bold letters that you put at the top of a slate which you want a pupil to copy. Peter says that Christ is our example, He died for us to show us how we can cope with suffering, hardship, adversity and persecution. He died for us as our substitute (which he expounds boldly and unforgettably in chapter 3), the just for the unjust that He might bring us to God; but He died also to show us how to live as Christians in the world. John: we all know John 3:16 and rejoice in its marvellous message. But what about 1 John 3:16? That too mentions the death of Christ, and it says something about our lives—'This is how we know what love is: Jesus Christ laid down his life for us. And we ought to lay down our lives for our brothers.' In other words, the death of Christ not only explains powerfully and persuasively why Jesus died, but how believers live.

I want us to come this morning to the first of these Passion narratives with that word of introduction, and to see that what Matthew is saying is that Jesus is the searching judge. All the characters who feature in the drama are in the dock. They are being judged by what they do and say, and also by their apathy—what they don't do and say. Matthew's Gospel may well have been written for a Jewish audience. In Matthew's dramatic introduction, the story of the advent, we read: 'You are to give him the name Jesus, for he shall save his people from their sins' (1:21)—Jewish people and Gentile people. And at the end of this marvellous Gospel this good news is to be proclaimed to the whole world: 'Go into all the world to every nation and announce the good news that sinners—sinners such as those that took Christ to His cross—can be most certainly forgiven' (cf. 28:19). Yes, of course it happened within a Jewish context, but because men and women are sinners, any other nation in the world would have done just the same, receiving the same kind of word from God.

We're all sinners, Matthew says, and right at the beginning of his Gospel he's saying that his message is for everyone. Wise men in its birth-narratives come from another country altogether, searching to find out who Jesus the king of the Jews is and where He was born. At the end of that chapter the baby Jesus is taken away to safety in another country to be sheltered and protected. And even in the birth-narratives where the story should be of joy and happiness and gladness, it's all stained by sin. He comes to save His people from their sins.

Sin's duplicity—Herod saying, 'When you've found Him bring me word so that I can come and worship Him also', when really he wanted word so that he could execute, not worship, Jesus.

Sin's consequences—Jesus taken away as a tiny babe by Joseph and Mary to another country, suffering, as refugees, because of sin.

Sin's enormity—the massacre of the innocents, every male child slain under the age of two. They were people totally uninvolved, but sin's like that. That's the awful, terrible thing about it, its appalling power to reproduce itself again and again in human life. And if you study carefully the distinctive parables recorded by Matthew you'll that they too have much to say about sin's hardness, proliferation, selfishness, resistance and arrogance. And it is certainly so in Matthew's Passion narrative.

Sin's anguish—it's Judas in this Gospel who says 'I have sinned!' It's Pilate in this Gospel who says 'I am innocent', as he plunges his hands into the basin. It's Jesus in this Gospel alone who, as He breaks bread at the table, says 'This is for the forgiveness of sins'—His life poured out for many for the forgiveness of sins.

Sin as greed

Surely one of the things that Matthew's Passion narrative is saying is that here you can see sin as greed. Here was a man who was prepared to sell his friend for money. Early in this same Gospel, the Sermon on the Mount carried such dire warnings of the awful, frightening danger of reckoning on the value of objects more than anything else. 'Do not lay up for yourselves,' Jesus said to Judas and to the others, 'treasures upon earth where moths and rust corrupt and where thieves break through and steal... Where your treasure is there will your heart be also' (cf 6:19).

Where was Judas's treasure? It was in the purse that John tells us about. He was a thief. He used to transfer money that didn't belong to him from the community purse to his own. And that's why Matthew, in his stark way, clearly links the glorious generosity of this unnamed woman (who didn't care about the cost, but knew that this might be her only chance, so she came with this precious casket because she wanted to show her love for Jesus) with Judas's greed. Matthew points out that at the moment Jesus is saying 'I tell you the truth, wherever this gospel is preached'—good news about His death because she'd done it to prepare Him for His burial—'what she has done will also be told, in memory of her' (26:13), at the same time—the tragedy of it!—'One of the Twelve... went to the chief priests and asked, "What are you willing to give me if I hand him over to you?" '

If only Judas had known, as he slipped through the streets that day finding his way to the chief priest's house, that whenever this message was proclaimed you'd hear about bad news, a man who would betray his closest friend just for thirty pieces of silver—the price of a slave, according to the law in Exodus 21. Do you know, Matthew heightens all this detail as no other Gospel writer does? He recalls the bargaining element—'What will you give me?' Nobody else tells you that. The woman in the house says, 'What could I give Him?' He says 'What will you give me?' And it's only Matthew who tells you how much it was: 'What's it worth?' It's worth the price of an unnamed slave. And it's only Matthew who actually spells out for you the horror of it—they counted it out for him. He wants you to see and feel it, the horror of it—'One: two: three: four: five... twenty-nine: thirty. That's your price'.

Matthew tells us that sin is greed. And not only individual greed but also collective greed. That's why they're so worked up about Jesus's prediction. 'He said, "I'm able to destroy the temple of God and rebuild it in three days".' the people said. It was the word of false witness. Why did they get so worked up? Recent sociological study of first-century Jerusalem has shown that between 40 and 45 percent of Jerusalem's inhabitants got their livelihood from the temple. They worked there, keeping it clean, dealing with its visitors, its administration, its preservation. So half the populace, when this word got around, were saying 'My money's at stake. If He's going to destroy this temple He's going to destroy my livelihood.' That's why they'll join their voices with others. 'This man puts my money at risk.' It's money that matters.

It's a very important theme for Matthew. Not only because Jesus taught it in Matthew 6: 'You cannot serve both God and Money' (6:24). Judas made the choice. When he left the room where the woman had spilled the ointment he was going to serve money. She wanted to serve God's Son. The narrative quite deliberately brings us to the parting of the ways.

And, my dear friends, it will not allow us just to condemn them. It will say to us, how much does money matter to *you*? It can matter too much. Of course we've got to live. But don't we live in a materialistic society, among people for whom things are everything? Make a bit more, go on in the rat race, and try to gain this and that which other people have got. Money matters: but we must make sure that it doesn't matter so much in our lives that we dishonour Jesus because of it.

That could be a high price for some to pay in contemporary society. It's not easy to ask somebody to cope with unemployment when the only option is a job that you are not too easy about as a Christian—perhaps because it's not using your gifts in quite the right way, perhaps because it involves persuading people to buy things which you know they can't afford, a kind of salesmanship that is not quite upright. But unemployment is a high price to pay for resisting it.

Jesus said, you must think of the woman. You must think about what pleases Christ. You must think about what honours Him. You must leave the issue, even of your everyday working life, in the hands of a God who loves you deeply and can only plan the best for you. Dear Christian friend, neither you nor I can possibly evade the warning of this passage. The individual who was greedy for gain came to see it was nothing. He took those same coins that had seemed so attractive as they were being counted out—but it was blood money. He didn't want it now, but other people didn't want to touch it either.

Money isn't actually all that precious. Its value is only relative. It can't be taken to eternity. Only the things that have been treasures in the heart and mind of Jesus will be over with us on the other side. Nothing else.

Are you rich toward God? How much have you got in your earthly bank balance? But what about your eternal investment, which might even—like this lovely woman's in the story—leave you somewhat poor in cash but rich in soul? Sin is greed. Is that saying something to someone here this morning? It always does to me. It's easy for the world around us, because it's so materialistic, to squeeze us into its own mould. It confronts us every moment on every advertisement hoarding, in every moment between items on the television screen—'You must have this! You must! This is life!'—when perhaps there are things that we ought to be doing for Jesus with the money we keep for ourselves.

She poured out the ointment which Jesus said would be talked of until eternity. Judas picked up his useless money. Sin is greed.

Sin as deceit

There are five aspects of deceit in this very chapter that is before us.

Matthew 26:4—the religious leaders are assembled together to discuss what they are going to do with Jesus. How are they going to handle this problem? An unusual prophet, a miracle-worker who is drawing crowds, a man who is making assertions about Himself offensive to their religious taste. But the discussion isn't all above board. They are looking to find out how to arrest Jesus 'in some sly way' so that they might kill Him. They don't want to conduct a fair investigation. They don't mind how they go about it.

Next Judas is exposed, in verse 25, as a deceiver as well as the priests and the scribes. You can understand the anguish of the group around the table when they hear that one of them will betray Jesus. 'Surely not I, Lord, surely not I'—but Matthew tells us, 'Then Judas, the one who would betray him, said, "Surely not I, Rabbi?" ' He'd already picked up the money!

In verse 59 the Sanhedrin were looking for false evidence against Jesus so that they could put Him to death. False evidence! The highest religious and moral court among first-century Jewish people; people whose lives in other respects, we have no reason to doubt, were morally upright. Certainly they possessed religious knowledge and theological convictions. Their own law, embedded eternally in commandments,

said 'You shall not bear false witness against your neighbour.'
Yet they were looking for false witnesses; pseudo-witnesses,
it means literally in the language in which this Gospel and the
others were first written.

Then these two pseudo-witnesses they discovered, after
they'd examined the claims of dozens and found them not
quite persuasive enough. Pseudo? Yes, but it must be *especially* pseudo if it's going to be convincing...

Then—sadness of all sadnesses—not just the enemies,
the traitor and the witnesses, but even a close follower. He'd
said, 'Everybody may betray You, but I won't betray You.'
Yet in the closing verses of this moving chapter he says 'I do
not know the man!' (verse 74). What appalling deceit!

My friends, before we condemn them: are we not sometimes guilty? Of saying the thing that we do not really mean,
of letting marvellous words in hymns slip easily from our lips?
'Take myself and I will be, ever, only, all for Thee'—then
somebody asks us to do some little thing for Jesus, and all the
other things that seem so important suddenly dominate the
scene. And what happens to the protestation of love and
loyalty—the exclusiveness of 'ever, only', the totality of 'all
for You'?

Sin as impulsiveness

Sin is impulsiveness. That's the third feature. Oh, not deliberate scheming, but sin which suddenly overtakes us in a
moment because we have to carry about this frail flesh of our
humanity and we're not perfect this side of heaven, nor ever
will be.

The impulsive word. Jesus has said to Peter 'This very
night... you will disown me three times' (26:34). And though
Jesus has said it earlier, Peter declares 'Even if I have to die
with you, I will never disown You.' It's not deliberate, it's
impulsive.

The impulsive deed, verse 51. One draws a sword and
strikes off the ear of the high priest's servant. If he'd thought
about it he would never have done it. How could he? John
tells us who it was; it was Peter. A man guilty of the impetuous word, the impulsive deed. Oh, he'd listened to the
words of Jesus and been persuaded by them. You must love

your enemies, must pray for those who despitefully use you...If somebody strikes you on the cheek you must turn the other one, not draw your sword—and he lacerates the face of this servant. He's been caught off-guard. How beautiful that it's in this same chapter that Jesus speaks at table about the forgiveness of sins! Not the sin of greed, materialism, deceit, sins of word as well as hand; but the sudden unexpected sins, the impulsive times when we say something which clearly can't be a true indication of what we really think and are. And when we do things that we know that if we'd had a moment to think about it, we wouldn't have done it—and we wish we hadn't. But how marvellous that Jesus says at this table, 'Drink from it [this cup], all of you. This is my blood of the new covenant, which is poured out for many for the forgiveness of sins' (26:27-28).

Sin as failure

There's a number of vivid Hebrew words used in the Old Testament to describe sin. One of them means 'missing the mark'. Sin's like that; knowing where you ought to aim but missing. And what a failure is described in this chapter.

The failure of the three in the garden. Jesus says 'Will you watch with Me? It's a dangerous moment. I long to be with My Father. Please help Me to pray with an undivided heart and mind knowing you are there. Please stay and watch with Me. My soul is overwhelmed with sorrow to the point of death. Stay here and keep watch with Me.' It was the last thing they could do for Him, but they failed Him. Just as we fail Him, sometimes when we certainly don't want to and wish we hadn't, but we do. Just as the three failed Him, as the twelve failed Him, as the one failed Him—'I don't know the man.' They all forsook Him, says Matthew, and fled.

Sin as unbelief

And sin is unbelief, expressed both in the courtroom and on the cross. I think this is one of the most important parts about Matthew's narrative and those of the other Gospel writers; because what people deny is the honour of Jesus, His names, titles and work. Unbelief is the worst sin of all. Not greed, not clutching the money; but failing to believe who Jesus is. And our belief, our trust and commitment to Him, is of the greatest importance.

There are six titles of Jesus, reflecting six aspects of His work, exposed in the courtroom and on the cross. And each becomes a subject for ridicule. Yet the whole of a Christian's believing life and experience is to be built on these great assertions.

First, (verse 61), *the temple of God*. Oh, they twist what He actually said. John tells us he said, doubtless pointing to Himself, 'Destroy this temple and in three days it will be raised again.' But they only half-hear it. They do not believe or even listen carefully to what He's trying to say to them. The temple was the place of revelation. And it wasn't in the future going to depend on a massive and impressive edifice in one particular part of the world. The revelation was going to be in a person, in Christ, the matchless Son of God. He was going to reveal God to men and women in a way that He had never been revealed so perfectly and uniquely before. But they rejected that destiny. The high priest said, verse 63, 'I charge you under oath by the living God: Tell us if you are the Christ.' The Greek word means 'anointed one'. The Hebrew word 'Messiah' means the same. Kings and priests were anointed to indicate their authority, that they were called by God to that particular office and must be respected for it. But they rejected His destiny as temple of God.

They rejected His authority, as *the anointed of God*. 'I adjure you, I'm placing you under oath, I'm solemnly demanding,' the high priest said, 'that you tell me if are you the temple of God, the anointed of God, the Son of God.' That's why Jesus replied. He could be silent when they said scurrilous things about Him but this was a moment for testimony. Earlier there'd been moments of testimony for Simon Peter. 'We believe that you are the Christ *the Son of God*.' And here it is the moment of testimony for Jesus. ' "Yes, it is as you say," Jesus replied.' But they rejected his authority.

They rejected his uniqueness as *prophet of God*. My friends, this has something to say to us. In this late twentieth-century world, a good deal of popular or at least media theology rejects the claims of Christ. In a pluralistic society, they are the offensive thing, not religion. 'But surely you accept that all religions in the end lead the same way?' It's the offence (called 'the scandal of particularity') of saying, 'There is no other name given among men whereby we must be saved, but the name of Jesus, the matchless Son of God.' But some religious leaders will say, 'Oh no, not Son of God in *that* sense. Perhaps He was adopted by God in some way and that title was an honorific one, a reward for leading a good life and saying good things.' That's not what Scripture says. Scripture says that Christian believers confess with gratitude their indebtedness to Christ the Son of God, who loved me and gave Himself for me. Unless He was God's Son on that cross, men and women are not saved. He was the prophet of God. They hit Him—'Prophesy to us, Christ!' You remember those words which John preserves at the beginning of the fourth Gospel—'Are you Elijah or Jeremiah, are you that prophet?' (cf. John 1:21). The special prophet with the capital P, the Prophet of Deuteronomy 18 who was to come into the world made like Moses, born among His brethren, saying unique things from God—you must listen to Him. But they rejected His uniqueness as prophet.

They rejected His message. And on the cross as He was dying for them and for all who would believe in Him, they took these treasured titles and continued with their ridicule and their mockery. They raised them again, the temple of God, the anointed of God, the Son of God, the prophet of God. 'Prophesy!' they said, 'and we will believe in you.'

And they took two more of His titles.

They said 'You are *the saviour of the world*', and ridiculed that. It's in this same Gospel that a group of terrified disciples in a boat tossed to and fro on a stormy lake, thinking that their own life was at an end, said 'Lord save us!' He is the Saviour. 'Come down from the cross' they said. They rejected His work. William Booth was right when he said, 'They said they'd believe if He came down. I believe because He stayed up.' Jesus knew there was no other way. He had to go through that experience of death until the moment of total and extreme desolation, when all His friends had gone and those who loved Him most had gone. And then in all the darkness even the Father turned His face away. 'My God, my God, why have you forsaken me?'

And they said 'You're *the king of Israel*, are you? You should be able to do anything if you are the king.' They rejected His supremacy. The worst of sins is unbelief.

Go through Matthew 26 and 27 sometime; you will that that's only the beginning of what Matthew has to say about sin. Sin is envy: Pilate saw that they wanted to arrest Jesus out of envy. Sin is cowardice: the Governor knows He is innocent, but plunges his hands into the basin. He hasn't the courage of his convictions. Sin is manipulation: the chief priests and the elders persuaded the people. The awful sin of using other people as things is not just a first-century sin, it's a twentieth-century sin as well.

The sin of derision, the sin of mockery. That's a twentieth-century sin; if you cannot accept Christ's deity you even deride His humanity, you make Him think things in the moment of death in that appalling film 'The Last Temptation of Christ' that even a decent man wouldn't be thinking about in a moment like that—sexual fantasies of one kind and another, when such a thought could never enter His pure and beautiful mind about people He loved. That is what it means to live in a sinful world. If you don't want to follow Him you don't want other people to follow Him either. Sin as derision.

Sin as blasphemy, sin as apathy: 'sitting down they watched Him there'. Sin as intransigence: even when He died they were picking up money. This time it's the soldiers being paid to keep quiet: 'remember...that deceiver said'—even when He died, this Gospel said, they described Him as a deceiver.

But I say to you, these sins and any others may all be forgiven, thank God, because of what Christ did for us on that cross; because He said in that last evening meal what Christian believers have proved to be wonderfully true. 'This is my blood of the new covenant poured out for many for the forgiveness of sins'.

Thanks be to God!

2. The Courageous Servant
(Mark 14:1–15:47)

We are looking this morning at Mark's account of the death of the Lord Jesus, and seeking to discover together by God 's Holy Spirit what he is saying to us, supremely of course about the suffering of our Saviour and why He died, but also about how we are meant to live for Him. I'm struck, in these chapters of Mark, by the way the RSV preserves that little word 'and'. There is a sombre note about it, a steady toll like a bell. One anguish, one pain upon another—'and...', 'and...', 'and...' There was something so desperately cruel and persistent and relentless in what was being done to Him. They were determined in every way possible to heap one indignity upon another.

Mark preserved that story, I deeply believe, because he wanted Christian believers to know the only way by which they could be forgiven: through the Christ who died for them, took their sins to His cross and bore them as their substitute and only Saviour, the one who stayed on the cross. In Mark's Gospel one miracle quickly follows another. If there is any Gospel which leaves you with a sense of stunned wonder at the power of Christ and all He is able to do in the lives of other people, it's this one. But here in the moment of His greatest physical and spiritual need, no miracle was going to relieve Him of suffering. The greatest miracle of all was waiting for Easter Day. He was to go through this suffering and be raised from the dead by the power and the glory of the

Father who loved Him and treasured Him from all eternity—
the Father who, in that awful moment as Jesus bore our sins
on that cross, turned His face away from His best-beloved
Son, so that He cried out, in the psalm that doubtless He had
treasured in His mind across the years and found comfort in
even on the cross: 'My God, my God, why have you forsaken
me?' (Psalm 22:1).

Mark wrote his story of the cross to tell how we can
become Christians. But I am also deeply persuaded that he
had another purpose which must not be dismissed. He did tell
us the story so that we could understand fully that Jesus died
as our substitute; but writing in a period of fierce persecution
he wanted Christians to understand, too, that it is costly to be
a believer. What Jesus said must be taken seriously. 'If any
man will be My disciple, he must take up his cross. It will not
be enough for him to kneel in gratitude at Mine. He must
follow in My steps, he must bear his cross. There will be a
price in his or her life that has to be paid. And to walk with
Christ is to walk the way of rejection and shame and derision
and scorn and ridicule.'

If New Testament scholars are right, there is every likeli-
hood that this Gospel was written first. There is every likeli-
hood that it was written in Rome, and that (if we can trust
Papias, an early writer about the Gospels) Mark became
Peter's interpreter. He was the writer, Peter the one who
supplied the details and the reminiscences.

It may have been written in the dark days of the persecution under the mentally deranged Nero. In 64 AD there was a
vast fire in Rome. Only four of the city's fourteen districts
escaped. Soon it was rumoured that the Emperor had started
it, which many had cause to believe. Nero, who was
extremely unpopular at the time, became worried. He put
the blame on the Christians, according to the writer Tacitus.
Tacitus had no love for Christians. But he disliked intensely
what had happened, because he said the blame was put on
believers because Nero wanted to escape it.

Nero fastened the guilt and inflicted the most exquisite tortures
on a class hated for their abominations, called Christians by the
people . . . mockery of every sort was added to their deaths. Covered with the skins of beasts they were torn by dogs and perished,

or they were nailed to crosses or they were doomed to the flames. They served to illuminate the night when daylight failed. Nero threw open his gardens for the spectacle while he mingled with the people in the dress of a charioteer and drove about in a chariot. Hence even for criminals who deserve extreme and exemplary punishment there arose a feeling of compassion, for it was not as it seemed for the public good, but to glut one man's cruelty that they were being destroyed.

Suetonius, another Roman historian, wrote: 'Punishment at that time was inflicted on the Christians, a class of men given to new and wicked superstition'; and Clement of Rome, a Christian writing later in the century, described the persecution of those grim days: 'Peter died, bore witness, proceeded to his due place in glory and Paul the same.'

I agree with those who believe that this Gospel belongs to that period. And in its pages Christians are reminded that it isn't easy to be a Christian; believers may have to pay a price. That's why the story is told so clearly and persuasively. Believers must walk the way of Christ, and that must mean essentially the way of the cross. They may not be called upon to die in that desperately cruel way, but to live for Jesus means that you will live under the cross. It will cost you something to be a Christian.

Mark is not saying this only in the course of his Passion narrative. He says it earlier in his Gospel too. He has a number of ways of driving the point home. He does so in the way he begins the story, because he points out in his opening paragraphs that one of the greatest people in the story of the coming of the Christ—John the Baptist—became a martyr. Mark, unlike the other writers of the Gospels, has very little to say about John's persuasive teaching. Right at the beginning he says that it was 'after John was put in prison', and the term he uses is the same as that describe the handing over of the Lord Jesus.

While Jesus was preaching the good news and calling on people to repent, there was a man who sat in the dark loneliness of a grim prison, with only the thoughts about his past, may we say it, immense success, and the awful feeling of desolation and occasional doubt that may creep over the spirit of any sensitive person. 'Is He the one who should come, or should we look for someone else? I don't see much evidence of the winnowing fan in His hand. In what way is the axe being laid to the root of the tree? People seem to be eager to hear His message, finding life in Him, enjoying Him and pleasing Him—but what about the message of judgement, the warning that I gave, surely from God, to those vast crowds of people?'

Mark has it at the very heart of his story in his sixth chapter, which describes this prisoner in great detail; how, strangely, he became quite popular with the king who had arrested him, yet had to pay the supreme sacrifice. Mark is here saying that if you want to speak boldly of the Christ, expose men's sins, point to the Lamb of God, tell of the power that will come into any human life through the ministry of God's indwelling spirit—there may be a price to pay. You will not always be surrounded by eager people anxious to drink in every word. There will be moments of desolation and pain. And so there have been for Christian believers; in the first century and all through those that followed, some had to pay the same price that men and women did in the persecution under Nero.

Mark tells us the story of John the Baptist to remind us that to be in the work of Christ is to be extraordinarily vulnerable. He says it not only of John, but of His own disciples, of all who are going to follow Him. You know those passages in chapters 8 and 10 well enough. Jesus says 'You must take up your cross, you mustn't be ashamed of Me. You must bear your cross in the world.'

He speaks about what it will cost. Many will give up houses and lands and popularity. They will receive so much from Jesus, but, as Mark alone points out (10:30), with persecutions. It was costly for John, it was costly for the disciples, it's costly for those who would be the first to follow Christ. Is it not especially significant that in Mark 13:9-13 Jesus speaks to His men about the difficulties that are going to come to them and to others when He has gone?

But it's also a description of what is going to happen to Him. He is anticipating His own cross as He is describing theirs. The happenings foretold in these verses happened to Him just as they happened to them. Surely it is a most brilliant and persuasive way of introducing us to this great theme that to suffer and pay the price as a Christian means to walk in the way of Christ. Jesus is not just describing something that might happen to them. He knows that it will. He says, 'You will have to follow in My steps. But I am not calling you to something I didn't have to suffer Myself. I know what it is to be in every one of those situations— handed over, flogged, standing before governors, arrested, brought to trial, made to confess, betrayed, hated. But you can stand firm, if you stand firm in Me.'

Jesus had said already in this Gospel (chapters 8-10) that these sufferings would come to Him. They did not take Him by surprise. You remember those passages where He gathered them around Him; though they were perplexed and bewildered, and Peter was even offended, Jesus said 'It's going to happen to Me. They will arrest Me, they will crucify Me. But on the third day I will be raised from the dead.'

In chapter 8 Peter can't accept it. In chapter 9 the disciples can't understand it, they're bewildered. In chapter 10 when they hear it they don't relate it to their life. In the immediacy of their situation, having heard all that about the pain and ignominy of it all, two of them are having a discussion about places of glory and prominence and dignity and position. They hear about the cross, but they do not apply it to their life situation.

In all these ways—by His sayings about John the Baptist, by His warnings about the cost of discipleship, by His description of the sufferings of those who would follow Him and of His own sufferings—Jesus is saying so persuasively by the Spirit through Mark, that those who would come to the cross for salvation must take up the cross for sanctification and in service.

How is it done? Well I want to suggest to you that in a variety of different ways Mark, the gifted first Gospel writer, takes these lovely stories and presses them home in such a way that Christian people who know that they are forgiven by the unique death of Christ, who've nothing to add to their salvation by their sufferings, must express their salvation by paying a price in one way or another.

Stuart Holden, a Keswick speaker many years ago, used to

say that nobody can truly be a Christian in the New Testament sense simply by saying that they are *just* relying on the blood of Christ. Oh yes, that is the way you become a believer; but if you want to live at your best for Jesus and be truly sanctified in the New Testament sense, the Lord Jesus will expect you to shed some of your own blood as well. Not so that you may be forgiven, but so that you may be like Him, so that people may see His beauty in you. And it will not be possible unless somewhere or other in your believing experience there is a price to be paid. A drop of blood, somewhere or other, will be shed.

But how are we to cope with that? We all love safety, peace, security, popularity, acceptance—so how are we to do it? I believe that Mark wants Christian believers to know that the way that Jesus walked and the features of His life and ministry and death are very special for Christians who are in times of trouble, suffering and pain.

I believe that's why at the beginning of his Passion narrative, on which Luke and others drew, he tells in chapter 14 a story about a woman who loved Jesus. This woman (whom we met yesterday) broke a very expensive jar of perfume and poured the perfume on His head. She knew it was a hostile atmosphere. That's how the chapter begins. The leaders were looking for some sly way to arrest Jesus and kill Him. He wasn't in any context a widely acclaimed popular figure by that time. There were people who were trying to hunt Him down.

Mark wants us to know, it wasn't something that happened just at the end. Why, right at the beginning of the Gospel, when He worked His earliest miracles, they tried to arrest Him, they wanted to kill Him. It didn't take Him by surprise. That's why time and again He gathered His men about them and told them about His sufferings and about theirs.

But what is the clue? How can you stand for Christ when it's tough, when there is a price to pay, when you're opposed and ridiculed and you hardly know where the strength is coming from—when you're encountering real hardship and adversity? Love is the key. It depends on how much we love Jesus. Right at the beginning of this narrative we are told about a woman who loved Him. She wasn't concerned about those who opposed and plotted against Him. She had something to bring to Him. She wasn't ashamed, but came boldly into somebody else's home. Though she was surrounded by others, she came to make her confession. She poured the anointing oil on His head.

Love absorbs criticism

The Old Testament prophets not only spoke and taught in words, but also sometimes presented the truth visually. I think that is what we have in this passage: one of the acts of 'prophetic symbolism'—saying something by means of an unforgettable visual aid, just as Jesus took a piece of bread and broke it at the last supper. *Christos* meant 'Anointed One'. She came boldly to make her confession of Christ and was criticised for it: only kings and priests were to be anointed. But Mark is saying that if we truly love Him, love will absorb criticism. They rebuked her harshly (14:5); they were not content to let her bring her gift, though it was her jar of perfume, she could do what she liked with her own money. They had other ideas about how the money might be spent. All through the centuries there have many who have told Christians that they could do better things with their time, their gifts, their energies and their money. There's nothing new here.

It's the beginning of confession; it's the beginning of a price that had to be paid.

She doesn't shed her blood; but she has to accept the rebuke and reproach of all the people around her. She's prepared to pay that price. In a way she is, right at the beginning of the Passion narrative, a model of what a true confessor of Christ should be like. She comes to make a personal confession, because she wants to, though she is surrounded by other people. She's not content to let others do it. She won't give her casket of perfume into the hands of another—somebody, perhaps, welcome at that table and known to the host—she does it herself, because personal confession must be made in that way.

It was not only personal, it was perceptive. She was doing it because she knew who He was and where He was going. He was going to His death. They anointed kings, but she knew they anointed corpses too; and she was going to do it now because in a few days there might be nobody else to anoint Him. But it was urgent; she had to make her confession then, for the moment might never return. She grasped the opportunity to let people know that she loved Jesus. Oh it was public; other people saw it. It was controversial; there were people who thought that the money could have been better spent. It was costly; Mark alone tells us that she broke the jar. She gave it all, decisively and finally. She didn't just give part of it, she broke the casket as she offered everything to Jesus.

And there was, too, something eternal about it. As Jesus saw what she did, He said 'She's done it against My burial. Wherever the good news is proclaimed in all the world, people will talk about men and women like this who make their confession, who say "You are the Anointed One—the Son of God, the true king, the priest who was anointed" '— the priest who felt for her, though people were criticising her—'Let her alone, she has done a beautiful thing for Me'—the priest who feels for us when people oppose us and say cruel things about us. He's not only the king who rules and reigns in His sovereignty and will do all things well even when things are tough, but He's the one who knows how we feel because He is touched with the feeling of our infirmity (cf. Heb. 4:14).

At the beginning of this matchless narrative Mark is saying, 'You must love.' If you want to be true to Christ, if you want to stand firm in time of persecution and adversity as the first readers of this Gospel were compelled to do, then most of all you must love Jesus and not be ashamed of Him. You will sometimes have to confess 'You are the Christ', not by breaking open a casket but by acknowledging Him as your king and your priest, who suffered and died for you, was buried and was raised from the dead for you. And you will be criticised for it.

The woman absorbs the criticism. She says nothing. She makes an outward confession in what she does, as she brings the best to Jesus: but she does not answer her critics. Love absorbs criticism! There are times, my friends, when we are opposed and the best response is not to answer back but to be serenely quiet.

If Papias is right and Mark is preserving Peter's reminiscences for us, we can understand why in his first epistle Peter wrote that when Jesus was reviled, He reviled not again (1 Pet. 2:23). 'He was not like me in the garden. When they reviled me I came back, cursing and swearing, but when they did that to Jesus He was silent at times when He knew it was essential to be silent'—and there are some times when you're criticised and ridiculed and the best thing you can do is just to be quiet.

Actually the Lord Jesus is often silent in Mark's Gospel. He only speaks three times in Mark's Passion narrative, and then only when compelled to do so. At other times Pilate, the priests and the governor are bewildered by His silence. Like the woman who loved Him, He thought it best to say nothing in certain circumstances. He was just quiet. And so must we be. Sometimes, of course, there will be an opportunity for you to speak, just as there were opportunities for Him. But love absorbs criticism.

Love welcomes truth

We come from the story of what happened in that room to the story of what happened in another: when Jesus gathered His disciples around Him in another act of prophetic symbolism; now not something done to and for Him, but something He does Himself. He takes a piece of bread and breaks it. No doubt a shudder went around the table. They knew exactly what He was doing. That kind of symbolism was not merely a visual aid, there was a sense among the Hebrew people that the sign could not be separated from that which was being symbolised. You were almost setting events in motion by breaking the bread: 'This is my body'.

Three times in Mark 14 Jesus says 'I tell you the truth': in verses 9, 18 and 25. What Jesus is saying is that love welcomes truth; if you are going through a period of pressure and persecution, you must listen to the truth. Jesus looked at His disciples and said, literally, 'Amen: I am the Amen...I say to you, you can depend upon Me, what I am saying to you is the truth.' You will only be able to endure persecution and suffer for Christ, you will only be able to live at your best in dark and difficult times, if your mind is stored with the truth. 'I tell you the truth!' Jesus says. That's why this matchless book is vital for us.

And what is the truth? As they sat around Him at that table at which He was going to break bread and pour out wine, He reminded them of the great truth: that it was Passover. Mark keeps repeating it, verses 12, 14, 16. 'I tell you the truth, this is Passover. This is a time for remembering with gratitude the power of God and all that God has done for our people in the past, delivering them from oppression, bringing them out of slavery, effecting for them miracles they cannot possibly work for themselves, changing them, transforming them. Remember,' Jesus says, 'I tell you the truth. This is Passover time, you must listen to the truth.'

The early Christians who read this story understood this: it's always Passover with God. He can come to us in our helplessness and frailty, just as the Hebrew people were helpless in Egypt; and He can always work for us transformingly. He can always give us power beyond ourselves, energy of which we would never be able to dream. Remember the power of God.

Remember the reliability of God; God is not only powerful, He is faithful. What was the language at the table? 'I tell you the truth, it's covenant time,' Jesus says. 'This is the blood of the covenant.' That was the agreement. This recalls Exodus 24, when the agreement was made. God made a promise with His people. And if God makes a promise and pledge with His people, He will never let them down. Jesus is not only speaking about the power of God to those at that table and to all who are about to suffer, but about the reliability, dependability and faithfulness of God.

And it's about the generosity of God, even to people who ridicule, revile, and say scurrilous things. Jesus says, 'This blood of the covenant which is poured out'—that would recall for them, lovers of the Old Testament that they were, the majestic words of Isaiah 53:12.

And it's about the mercy of God, and about the victory and power of God, as Jesus points them forward by telling them the truth of great and better things that were yet to be.

'I tell you the truth, I will not drink again of the fruit of the vine until that day when I drink it anew in the kingdom of God' (14:25). God in His sovereignty would bring Him and all believing people to victory. It wouldn't all finish in that desperate moment when they took His body down from the cross. There would be Easter Day, and the day would come when He would drink anew in the kingdom of God, when all who loved Him would come, many of them through suffering and pain and anguish and derision and ridicule—the way of the cross; but the way to the throne, to the banqueting hall of the Lamb of God—until we drink it anew in the kingdom of God. 'But I tell you the truth,' Jesus says, 'love absorbs criticism, but love welcomes truth.'

Love expresses gratitude

But you must also be thankful. In your darkest hour you must think about something for which you can give thanks. At that table (verse 22), 'while they were eating Jesus took bread, gave thanks.' Fancy saying thank you in a moment like that! The very breaking of the bread would tear asunder the soul of a sensitive person, as the majestic Son of God most certainly was. 'This is my body'—but He could say thank you, in His darkest hour. Why? What did He want to say thank you for?

In that moment, surely, He wanted to thank God that He had lived the life for Him. He gave thanks, He took a piece of bread. Of course it was Passover, but as He looked at the bread before it was broken He thanked God that the bread had been given—life for the world, before it had been broken on the cross. The bread had been served generously. He had given His life in service before He came to give it in sacrifice.

As He looked around the table He may have given thanks for the disciples. Luke tells us He said to them in His darkest hour 'You are those who have been with Me in My tribulation as you have been My partners.' He gave thanks for what was going to happen through the breaking of that bread. Surely He did not just look into their pained faces. In that moment He knew what was going to happen through the breaking of that pure and lovely body; that there would be not scores, not hundreds, not thousands, but millions through the centuries who would come to personal faith in Him. Yes, Jesus could look at the cross and know all the pain of it, yet look beyond it to greater and more wonderful things. He gave thanks for those who would yet believe, that He would see of the travail of His soul in the sovereignty of God and be satisfied; that He would see men and women like you and me, who through the shedding of that blood alone can come to personal faith in Christ and certainty and confidence in God; so that knowing you belong to Him, no matter how tough your situation, you are given the strength to endure—as Jesus says—to the end.

Love recalls mercy

After the meal, 'when they had sung a hymn, they went out to the Mount of Olives' (verse 26). We can say almost certainly what the hymn was that He encouraged them to sing. It would have been one of Psalms 115-118, the *Hallel* psalms that were sung at the close of Passover meals by the Hebrew people.

Jesus does not only point the disciples forward. He points them back. When Paul and Silas were imprisoned in Philippi while following this way of the cross, having been arrested, ridiculed and lashed they were put in chains in a dungeon. What did they do? They sang a hymn, it says, to God. Doubtless they reminded themselves of the great words of Scripture. They sang a hymn, perhaps one of those that have been briefly but beautifully preserved within the pages of the New Testament. It's a reminder that when you are in great trouble, don't only look at the trouble and beyond it to the moment when it will be over; think too of the past, sing a hymn.

If you look at Psalms 115-118 you'll realise how wonderfully appropriate they are. Psalm 115: God is reliable. Psalm 116: God is near. Psalm 117: God will hear you. Psalm 118: God has helped you; He has helped all His people and He will go on to help you. They sang because they thought of the goodness and greatness of God in the past.

Love renews confidence

Mark takes us now into the garden. Jesus has asked if He can be alone in the place of prayer. In the time of persecution and adversity, that was saying something very deep and profound, wasn't it? It is a reminder to Christians called upon to suffer, not only to sing a hymn and remind themselves of the goodness and greatness of God in the past—we should do that, and realise He won't let us down—but to go into a quiet place and say, 'Father'.

Confidence in the Father: only Mark records the lovely name that Jesus used: 'Abba, Father'. When it's really difficult and you don't know where the strength is coming from, just kneel and say 'Father'. That's what Jesus did. 'Not My will, not what I want. Everything is possible to You; but not My will but Yours be done.'

Confidence in Scripture: that's one of the things this passage is affirming. Like all Mark's accounts, it's full of Old Testament references. The Lord Jesus has just quoted Zechariah 13—'I will strike the shepherd and the sheep will be scattered.' The Son of Man will be taken and arrested and ridiculed, just as it was predicted about Him. He's reminding them of Scripture. Take the word of God as Jesus took it, and feed on it and be sustained by it.

And lastly, confidence in the future; looking ahead to the day when things would be different, when He would drink anew in His Father's kingdom.

Love receives strength

From this point on in the narrative, it seems that in a variety of different ways the readers of this matchless story—the early Christians especially, who were called upon to suffer—are being reminded of a number of Jesus' experiences, to see how He suffered and endured, and how He through and in the power of Christ and by the Spirit could be firm to the end. It's how love receives strength. It's how you're fortified.

And it's how the Lord Jesus was the matchless hero. It's about the heroism of Christ, doing the Father's will, saying 'Not My will but Yours be done', walking this way of the cross, knowing that what He did for them there upon that cross, no other would have to do. By that death alone they would be redeemed, so that others would follow Him. It would be the way of their service and the way of their sanctification. And they would be given courage when danger approached, when it was a hard price to pay.

Notice how Jesus, after the singing of the hymn and the prayer in the garden declares: 'The hour is come. The Son of Man is betrayed into the hands of sinners. Rise! Let us go! Here comes my betrayer!' He does not shrink from it but goes out confidently, heroically, courageously. Many who followed Him would know that same courage in approaching danger. There would be later informers and betrayers all through Christian history. And Jesus, the one who would uniquely die for their salvation, said, 'Don't let's face danger and persecution as if we were terrified by them. Arise! Let us go!

Courage in approaching danger—and courage in hurtful treachery. The betrayer is coming through the crowd to kiss Jesus, just as many afterwards would be betrayed by people they thought loved them. Courage, too, in extreme loneliness: 'Then everyone deserted him and fled' (verse 50). There was no one round Him now to sing those great Hallel Passover hymns; not even three friends trying helplessly to protect Him in the corner of the garden. They'd all gone, He was alone, as many others would be through the centuries.

And courage under repeated interrogation; questions were hurled at Him, just as they would be to Christian believers during the Neronian persecution and later on throughout history, some in our own time. God forgive us when we are sometimes silent, when we are cowards, when it may only cost us a blush: for many brave brothers and sisters the cost is their blood.

Jesus showed courage for bold confession. There was a time to be quiet under ridicule and hostility, and a time for bold confession too: 'Yes, I am the Christ, the Son of the blessed one and the Son of Man who will most certainly come on the clouds of glory.' And courage in repeated derision, when they mocked Him and hit Him, saying 'Prophesy!' as they struck Him. Luke preserves the detail for us: 'We've hit you. Well now, tell us. You're blindfolded: if you're a prophet you ought to be able to name the person who hit you' (cf. Luke 22:64). But even in their ridicule they didn't realise that even in those moments He was exercising a prophetic ministry. He was speaking the truth.

Of course, He was predicting the coming glory of the Son of Man. But His prophetic word was also being unfolded even down there in the courtyard. He had told one of His disciples that before the cock had crowed three times, he would deny Him thrice: it was being fulfilled. He had reminded them of Zechariah 13, the prophecy that the shepherd would be smitten and the sheep scattered: it was being fulfilled at that very moment—most of them were hiding in the dark, safe corners of Jerusalem. 'Woe unto that man by whom He is betrayed', He had said—and in those moments a man who had the money in his purse was stricken with remorse and appalling guilt.

He was the prophet even though they ridiculed Him. He was making His bold confession. And surely it's not without significance that the narrative juxtaposes Jesus—making His bold confession, showing how to judge when it is appropriate to speak and when to remain silent, how to speak for Him— with the man down in the courtyard, showing how not to do it—cursing, swearing, denying, forsaking. Jesus showed his courage in sustained silence.

Courage, too, when they put Him on the cross in agonising pain. That's why I prefer the RSV—'and they did this to Him... and they did that to Him'. Mark observes that they offered Him the customary myrrhed wine to deaden the pain. But He refused it. He wanted an unclouded mind as He went on to that cross, to think clearly about what they were saying around Him, about people who might call to Him—as the thief in Luke's account does—for help; about the woman who (as John records) stood near and the disciple whom He loved—He wanted and longed that he might become her son in the future.

He didn't want to be made soporific by that wine (a merciful touch probably provided by the women of Jerusalem). He refused to take it because He wanted a clear mind to think about the needs of others, to be able to speak with the Father, to be able to think about those words in

Psalm 22 and other psalms. And He wanted a clear mind to hear some of the things being said to Him, for even in their ridicule there was a note of comfort. 'After three days He will raise this temple up'—three days later, on the way to glory, He received strength for the agonising pain, and he received courage in apparent failure. 'He saved others but He cannot save Himself!'

This Gospel is so crowded with miracles. Yet He denies Himself a miracle because He waits for a greater miracle of resurrection, that will be a type of the greater miracle that will happen in the future. Those who are dead in their sins will be raised to newness of life in Christ.

Most of all, He received courage in spiritual bewilderment. Those bewildering times when you feel that even God has left you—the Father turned His face from Him as He bore our sins: 'My God, my God, why have you forsaken me?' I'm sure in my own mind that Mark's account of the Passion was written primarily of course to point his readers to their Saviour, but also to point them too to their Hero, the sufferer who died for them, who went through this persecution and adversity, but leads them on to the way of glory.

And that's why at the end of this account Mark points out for us two brave and perhaps surprising people: a brave soldier who has the confidence to say 'Yes, He is the Son of God', and a man who bravely goes to beg for the body of Jesus. Mark tells us (verse 43) that Joseph of Arimathaea went boldly to Pilate.

A soldier who demonstrated publicly by his words that he belonged to Christ: and a rich Jew. 'There's something I can do to show that I belong to Jesus, I don't mind who knows. I know the whole Sanhedrin have condemned Him. I may be the only one!' He goes out boldly to make his confession.

And the two of them, the soldier and the rich prosperous Sanhedrin member become the first of millions who are willing to say 'Yes: because I love Him, because He's done everything for me. I too will break my casket, I will give Him everything. And I will show it by what I say as I make my confession, whatever it costs—"Truly He is the Son of God"—even though for some the cost is their lives. And I will show it not only by what I say but by what I do for Him. I will show that I belong to Him, and I love Him, and I am His for ever.'

3. The Compassionate Redeemer
(Luke 22:1–23:56)

We come to Luke's special message to us about the cross. I have tried to emphasise in these Readings something of the individuality of these 'Passion narratives'. It is fascinating to see how one particular writer with his own personal background and interest and understanding of the events shares distinctive things with us about the story. The writers of the Gospels were all very different men. The Lord in His great goodness takes people with different qualities and gifts and backgrounds and expertise. We're not all the same, thank God for that! We bring different contributions.

Matthew had been a tax collector, handling money day after day until Jesus came to his booth and asked him to leave his money and follow Him. Maybe that's why Matthew was particularly sensitive: he knew that money was a very dangerous, though a necessary commodity. Like Judas he had been a thief like all tax collectors were, putting the bare minimum—road tax or land tax or whatever—into the Roman box, and slipping a good amount (as everybody knew) into his own pocket.

Mark? Well, I believe Mark was the young man who was present at Jesus' arrest, wearing only a linen garment around him, and that when Mark described how everybody forsook Him and fled, he is surely identifying himself. One can't dogmatise, of course, but what a strange detail to include otherwise! Is it the signature of the artist, inscribed in a dark corner of the picture? Is he perhaps saying, 'I failed, just as Peter failed, just as the other disciples failed; but just because you fail once or several times, it doesn't mean to say that you can't at the last be a hero conquering through the power of Christ, and a disciple who'll follow Him steadfastly right to the end of one's days'?

Luke, I believe, was a particularly gifted writer. In saying that I don't in any way underestimate the qualities of the others. But Luke was one of those people who crowded a whole range of gifts and activities into his life. You do meet people like that sometimes, who seem so extraordinarily gifted. Luke was a skilled doctor who accompanied Paul on his journeys; and there must have been many times when Paul was grateful for Luke's partnership—not only writing the second volume, the Acts of the Apostles, but actually accompanying him and his colleagues. You remember those passages where Luke notes '*we* came to such and such a place.' Luke was actually present when it all happened. And how grateful Paul must have been for his gifts and skills as a doctor when he had been stoned and had wounds that needed treatment, when he was whipped (as he was at Philippi) and there was somebody there to care for him.

But Luke wasn't just a doctor. He was a very gifted historian. We know that from the Gospel and the Acts of the Apostles: the careful eye for accuracy, wanting to state the facts; here's reliable material. And he was a marvellous story-teller too. Not all historians are. Some very gifted historians are masters of collecting and sifting, but if you go and listen to them you've never been so bored in all your life. Luke wasn't like that. He was a marvellous raconteur, a brilliant story-teller of compelling skill.

Some people can tell a story, but they can't put it in writing. Luke was a brilliant writer. We have an enormous amount of Lucan material in the New Testament; more in fact than Paul's writings. This Gospel and the Acts of the Apostles are a two-volume work, a massive contribution by a brilliant writer inspired by the Holy Spirit.

He was also a very gifted and perceptive theologian. He knew the facts of the Gospel, those truths by which alone the

Christian church could be sustained through dark and difficult times. So he's not just detachedly telling a story; he's proclaiming some of the great truths of the Christian faith by which alone we can mature into strong Christians, and by which truths alone we can stand fast for Jesus in time of difficulty.

He knew the ancient world from his travels and his medical work. A doctor's work brings you into contact with all kinds of people; the extremely poor and the very rich. Luke knew not just about the aches and pains of the first century, he knew all about people and what made them tick, their lives, their background and so on. If I had the privilege of choosing one person in the life of the early church with whom to spend an evening, it would be Luke. He was so gifted. And especially so, I believe, in compiling this Gospel.

The Gospel writers have such different styles. Matthew the first-century tax collector was used to cooking the books, but he also had to keep the books. He was an orderly writer and his Gospel is orderly.

Mark has a racy style. He's always pushing you on to the next thing. A word that he uses again and again is one we translate 'immediately'. By the end one's quite breathless. He has a sense of urgency to go out and witness for Christ and follow Him. 'Don't be put off as I was put off once,' he says.

But Luke, I think, brings literary artistry, the extraordinary ability to paint marvellous pictures within just a phrase or two. And I want to suggest to you this morning that in Luke you have pictures of the Passion and they are pictures of Jesus. Of course you need Matthew's Gospel—the exposure of sin, to show us why the cross was necessary and why we must keep coming to Him every single day day for forgiveness. And we need Mark's Gospel, because of his emphasis on heroism and what he says about how Jesus endured. What are the things that kept Him going through His darkest hour, an hour darker than we would ever have to go through? Mark shows us how (as Peter put it) we can follow in His steps.

But you can't follow unless you look at Him. You must have a vision of Jesus, a big portrait of Christ. I believe Luke is creating an 'art gallery' of portraits of Jesus. And I want us this morning to come into it.

Luke presents these portraits with details not found in any other Gospel. He introduces us to completely new material. If you look at these narratives again later, as I hope you will, you'll find that there are between twenty and twenty-five details not found in the other Gospels; extraordinary detail that's all part of our total understanding of the message of the cross, but which we owe entirely to the gifted doctor and historian and theologian, inspired as he was by the gracious Spirit of God.

The portrait of the grateful partner

First of all, please turn with me to chapter 22, where Luke provides us with the detailed conversation of Jesus at the table. There are distinctive elements in it. Luke not only reminds us of the cup of the new covenant, but he deals with the disciples' responses. They begin to question among themselves who might be the one to betray Jesus, and the other writers record that too. But Luke notes a most astonishing thing. When (verse 24) they were talking about who was the worst, they started to talk about who was the best. What an extraordinary moment in which to have a discussion about who was the most important person among them! Luke tells us in his Gospel that this is not the first time that they had had that conversation. They had had it earlier, in Luke 9:46. On that occasion the Lord Jesus took a little child and put it in their midst. You would have thought that would have silenced them for ever, but no; at the table when the question is buzzing round, 'Who could the betrayer be?', 'Who is the worst?', they start to talk about who might be the best.

So Jesus has to speak to them again. The disciples are not seen at their best either here or earlier. But right at the heart of all that situation, when the disciples are not portrayed as a strong band of supportive brothers who can say to Jesus, 'We've sought to be obedient to Your teaching and followed You, and we'll stand with You'—Luke preserved a most beautiful little detail. Jesus not only gave thanks to the Father; He said thank you to them. 'You are those who have

stood by me in my trials [or testings or temptations]' (22:28).
What a lovely thing to say! He knew that they had failed Him
so desperately in the past, as we see for example in chapter 9
where He spoke of going on to His death, but they were dull
of understanding, they didn't understand, they were ignorant
about His mission on earth (9:44-5). They were arrogant
(9:46), insular (9:49), and loveless (9:52-56).

The disciples were not exactly supportive, model, close
followers of the teachings of Jesus. And yet He looked into
their faces on that last night, the night that He was betrayed,
and said to them so gratefully 'You are those who have stood
by me in my trials and testings and temptations.' He knew
their past mistakes, He knew their present failings—they
were arguing at the table. It was not only what they had
done, in Luke 9 and elsewhere, but what they were now
doing: having an argument. He's said so much to them about
the need for humility and trust in God, and here they are
asserting themselves even at the table. And it was what they
were going to be. He knew they were all going to forsake
Him and flee. And yet He said to them, 'You are those who
have stood by me in my trials.'

So here is Luke's first picture of the Passion of Christ. It
shows the Lord Jesus as the grateful partner, the one who for
all their mistakes and sins didn't just point their failings out to
them. He did so, kindly and lovingly. You've got to love
somebody very much to point out their errors, and they've
got to love you a lot if they are going to be able to take it. But
He also told them about the good and lovely and kind things
they'd done for Him. Luke's temptation narrative in chapter
4 says that the devil departed from Him after the temptations, when He was alone in the wilderness with no disciples
to stand alongside Him; the devil, says Luke, departed from
Him just for a season waiting for an opportune time to
return. And this little verse 22:28 tells us that the devil did
return, with temptations and tribulations time and time
again. But the Lord Jesus looked into the disciples'
bewildered faces that night and said to them, 'I'm so grateful
to you that you have stood by Me, you have been My partners, you have been My colleagues in dark and difficult days.'

My friends, Luke wanted to say that. I believe he was

meant to say it because of the pressure of the Holy Spirit in his heart and in his mind. But the early Christians had to work together in teams or everything would be lost. They weren't going to win as individuals, it was only as partners, and only then when they recognised that God was not likely to give them perfect partners; He hadn't given perfect partners to Jesus. But they must be ready to appreciate the good and kind things in their partners and not just constantly, meticulously point out their errors. The Lord Jesus is their model.

It's been said that appreciation is the lubricant of life. Do you say thank you to people who do things for you, or are you guilty at times of taking them for granted? The Lord Jesus was a grateful partner.

What Jesus is saying about partnership is very important. The verb translated 'stood by me' refers not just to the past but to the present. Jesus is saying, even in that moment when they were trembling on the threshold of defection, 'I'm grateful for this moment, you are standing by Me in my trials and testings.'

The portrait of the sensitive intercessor

The marvellous thing is that not only did Jesus recognise that they had stood by Him, He was going to stand by them.

In 22:31 Jesus turns from the group and speaks to one person: 'Simon, Simon, Satan has asked to sift you' (the word is plural, it means 'sift you *all*'). 'Simon, I am talking to you personally because what I am about to say concerns you. But it doesn't only concern you. Satan has desired to sift you *all* as wheat.'

In 22:3 of this chapter Luke records that Satan entered into the heart of Judas. And Jesus is saying that Satan is not content; the enemy of souls, the adversary, has his hands on Judas but he wants them all, to toss them like winnowing wheat so that in the end he can scatter and spoil and ruin them. Judas, poor man, is going to his place of eternal ruin, but if Satan had his way you would all be going with him. 'But I have prayed for you, Simon' (and now the word is singular) 'that your faith may not fail. And when you have turned back, strengthen then your brothers' (verse 32)—those who will also find themselves tossed about, going through trials and tribulations, needing people to stand by them and support them and be partners with them. The sensitive intercessor, Jesus, is telling Peter what He'd been praying about and who He'd been praying for.

It's one of the many cases in these Passion narratives where some of the writers' favourite themes. There's no sense in which the story of the cross is a block of material, however wonderful, tacked on the end of each Gospel. These narratives take up some of the great themes of the earlier parts of their Gospels. It's true with Matthew as I briefly demonstrated, and it's true with Mark, and so now with Luke.

Luke is a Gospel of prayer. It's Luke who tells you that when Jesus was baptised He was praying, who tells you in chapter 9 that it's as Jesus was praying that He was transfigured. In Luke 11 there is marvellous teaching about prayer. And there are parables about prayer like that of the importunate widow in chapter 18. Jesus is saying, 'I'm not just teaching you about prayer. I'm doing it, for you.'

I want to suggest to you nine features of prayer that Luke deliberately introduces and distinctively introduces into his Passion narrative. First,

The consolation of prayer
The first and most marvellous thing about prayer is that Jesus does pray for us. He encourages you to pray because when you come to the place of prayer, He prays for you.

This story is not told to tell the early church that at a particular moment Jesus prayed for Simon Peter. Not at all. Luke's a theologian. He knows the great truths that the apostle Paul and others sought to communicate, about the high-priestly ministry of Jesus. He knows that great truth which is taught in the matchless letter to the Hebrews, that 'He ever lives to make intercession for us' (Hebrews 7:25).

It's fascinating that it is in the New Testament writings addressed to persecution situations that the high-priestly ministry of Jesus is extolled. It's in the closing verses of chapter 8 of that majestic letter to the Romans, where you read about how He intercedes for us. It's in the letter to the Hebrews—written to Christians, if I understand it aright, who were in great danger of giving up under pressure. It's in the opening of the Book of the Revelation, the picture of the Lord Jesus in incomparable beauty, the portrait *par excellence* in the New Testament, where He is clothed with a garment reaching to His feet (Rev. 1:13) which was how priests were dressed.

The early church was being reminded that Jesus was praying for them. And this verse would encourage many a Christian in dark times—'I have prayed for you.' He is praying for us all, that's the miracle and wonder of it. Your name has been mentioned in Glory today. You say, that's humanly impossible! Of course it is—humanly. But we're not talking about merely human things. You are treasured in Heaven.

The realism of prayer

Look again at 22:33-34. Jesus prayed for Peter because He knew the pressures that he was going to go through as well as those He Himself was to go through. 'So I prayed for you and I know I must pray for you,'—the realism of prayer—'that your faith will not fail.'

The prayer was answered. Peter's courage failed, but not his faith, not as Judas abandoned his trust in Jesus. He was brought to the place of penitence and forgiveness and renewed grace and mercy. And he did stand up and strengthen his brethren. The prayer of Jesus was beautifully and gloriously answered. There were scores of churches all over Asia Minor that received Peter's first letter and second letters. Thank God that in that way they were being strengthened. Yes, the prayer of Jesus was being answered. But the realism of prayer is that you need to pray. Jesus prays because He knows the tough things that we're going to go through.

The discipline of prayer

Verse 39 refers back to 21:37. It speaks of the rhythm and pattern of this last week of the Lord Jesus's life. The Lord Jesus lived a disciplined, structured life. Of course He had time for the person who intruded into His programme. Love demanded it, and of course the One who loved us more than all others had time for the intruder. But that didn't mean He had no shape or design to His time. The rhythm of his day is given in 21:37. He taught during the day and climbed up into the hill at night. Why? To pray. Not just to rest, but, in that crucial time, to spend time with God to pray for Peter that his faith would not fail; to pray for the others, to pray for those who would despitefully use Him; to pray that He would know that strength that all His disciple had been promised for the future. He prayed.

He went 'as usual' to the Mount of Olives. That's exactly the same phrase that Luke uses in 4:16, 'as was His custom'. Jesus had a shape to His day and His week.

The discipline of prayer! Many a prayer life fails simply because it just isn't organised. There isn't shape. If the Lord Jesus had to plan His day to be at His best for His Heavenly Father, do you think we can just get through by snatching this moment and that, whenever we think it might be right for us?

The universality of prayer
Do you see what Luke is doing in verse 40? 'On reaching the place, he said to them...'—words that in the other Gospels are related to the three, Peter James and John. But Luke wants us to know that prayer isn't for the favoured few. The call to prayer was to all the disciples. He's reached the place; He says to all of them, 'Pray, all of you, that you will not fall into temptation.' The eleven were in need of this word of exhortation about prayer. I believe that after He'd said it to them all, He took the three along with Him, tenderly hoping that they would stand by Him in His trial and tribulation, and then said to them again, 'Now you must pray too. Pray, pray, pray, all of you.' The universality of prayer: it's for everybody, not just for the three.

The urgency of prayer
Look now at verse 46. The Lord Jesus is urging His disciples to get up and pray. He's saying to them at the end what He said to them at the beginning: 'Why are you sleeping?' They haven't realised that the hours and minutes are ticking away.

Oh of course it's necessary to sleep. You must have rest for your body, that's God's provision for you. But there are times in life when there are more important things even than sleeping, when it may be right not to sleep at that particular moment but to use that time for prayer.

There would be other times for sleeping. 'Pray so that you will not fall into testing.'

The partnership of prayer

Luke alone preserves the detail in verse 41. 'He withdrew about a stone's throw from them, knelt down and prayed.'

He'd asked them to pray, hadn't He? Right at the beginning, all the eleven, not just the three: 'All of you pray.' He'd expected them to pray. He withdrew just a little way to pray to pour out His heart in anguish to His Heavenly Father. Oh, the very prospect of that—bearing your sin and mine, and the sins of the whole world, in that pure and lovely and blameless and spotless body.

But He hoped that they would pray. They weren't praying, they were sleeping, but Jesus was only a stone's throw away. He didn't go too far from them, He was close to them. Nobody will shake my conviction that this is Luke's brilliantly artistic way of saying to us, 'If you do go to the place of prayer Jesus is only a stone's throw away.'

When you talk about somebody being 'only a stone's throw away', they are near enough to be seen. You wouldn't dream of saying that Penrith is a stone's throw away from Keswick, it would be ludicrous. The phrase means a very short distance away, near enough to be seen, near enough to be heard, near enough to be reached. He wasn't going to go far away. He knew they'd stood by Him, but He knew He had to stand by them in these perilous moments.

When you come to pray, the partnership of prayer is there. You enter into fellowship with the Lord Jesus. He's closer to us when we pray. He's only a stone's throw away.

The strength of prayer

Mark tells us that in the trials and temptations at the beginning, the angels came and ministered to Jesus. Matthew records for us Jesus' words when He was arrested, that battalions of angels were waiting to come down to stand by Jesus if He but called. But they were not summoned, because the Lord Jesus knew that the way of the cross was the way of sacrifice, the essential way of salvation. But now (verse 43) not a battalion but a single angel came alongside Him.

The word means 'messenger', it's a celestial messenger

from God. I believe in angels. Do you? In the first chapter of
the letter to the Hebrews, written to people exposed to
persecution and undergoing trials, the author speaks of
angels in relation to the Lord Jesus and His matchless
supremacy; but (verse 14) he says that those angels are ministers of salvation, servants sent to us. Many of the times
you've been rescued, guarded and protected were, if you but
knew it, because angels were there to help you. Perhaps some
accident might have been much worse. Perhaps there was
some temptation so strong that you hardly know how you
resisted it. The angels were ministering to you. It was some
accident that was bad enough but it might have been desperate if you only knew it, but for the angels. There was some
fierce moment of temptation and you were kept back and you
scarcely know how, there was some pressure upon your
spirit. The angels were ministering to you.

The intensity of prayer
Verse 44: 'Being in anguish, he prayed more earnestly.' This
is the same word used by Peter in his first chapter: more
earnestly, deeply. It's the same word that Peter uses in his
first chapter of his letter when he says, 'Love one another
deeply, from the heart' (1 Pet. 1:22). In that moment the
intensity of His prayers for His disciples appeared like drops
of blood. The word is *thrombos*, from which we get the word
'thrombosis'. The agony and the anguish and pain of it all!

The priorities of prayer
Jesus shows us, and Luke with his matchless artistry records
for us, what the priorities of prayer really are. He does so by
three uses of the name 'Father'.
    In verse 42 He prayed in the garden as He looked at that
cup—the anguish, the pain, the *thrombos* of it, bearing the
world's sin in His own pure body. But He said, 'Father—I
don't want to please Myself, I've only come into the world to
do Your will; and I'm going to do it now, and I say, not My
will but Your will be done.' The first priority of prayer is *to
offer ourselves*. It's not what we ask, it's what we give, it's
how we trust. 'Father, not my will but yours be done.'
    The second use of 'Father' is in the following chapter
(23:34). It is the first thing Jesus said when they drove in the

nails. As they nailed Him to the cross, the first thing that He
said was 'Father, forgive them, for they do not know what
they are doing. They don't realise the horror of this crucify-
ing the Son of God, the Lord of Glory. They've no idea what
they are doing.' This is the second priority of prayer: *to
pardon others*. Because if we come into the presence of God
with bitter feelings in our hearts, we will not be heard. Our
prayers cannot find that open entrance in the presence of a
holy, loving and just God if we are harbouring some bad
thought in our hearts and minds.

He, of all people, could have thought unkind things at that
desperate moment as they crucified Him. But He said
'Father, pardon others, forgive them, they don't know what
they're doing.' That's why the first martyr of the Christian
church, whose story Luke tells in the Acts of the Apostles,
follows in the footsteps of Jesus. They hurled those great
stones at him and accused him of blasphemy; and Stephen
knelt down and prayed just like Jesus: 'Lord, do not hold this
sin against them' (Acts 7:60).

The third time Jesus prayed and said 'Father' was in 33:46.
The curtain of the temple had been torn in two and He cried
out 'Father, into your hands I commit my spirit.' That's the
third priority of prayer. It's *to trust God*. He was quoting
from another Psalm: just as the quotation from Psalm 22 is
recorded in the other Gospels, here Jesus quotes from Psalm
31:5—'Into your hands I commit my spirit.'

The essentials of prayer are not the things we keep on
asking for. He wants us to ask, of course, but what are the
priorities? You see, if we have the priorities right then we will
be asking for the right things. If you can say 'Father, not my
will but Yours be done', then you're not anxious to collect a
whole range of additional possessions; what matters most for
you is the will of God. You're content with the Father's will.
If you pardon others (the second priority), you will pray for
others, for those who don't like you, who are unkind to you,
who are cruel. That will transform your attitude to them
when you meet them. The sad thing about broken relationships is that you find them where Christians have not prayed
for each other. If they had, it wouldn't happen.

The third priority: to trust God. In the most bewildering

and painful experiences of life to simply say, 'Father, I'll just put it into Your hands. Into Your hands I commit my spirit.' The Lord Jesus was on the threshold of death, facing the journey we shall all make unless the Saviour comes and takes us in triumph to Himself. What will we say when we face that journey? There's only one thing you can say. 'Our Father.' There's nothing to worry about. You're just a little child in the hands of a father. Those of you who are parents would never dream of doing anything but the best for your dear children. The children are safe with you, aren't they? Of course they are! You love them more than you love yourself. Well, that's what the Father says to us. At the end you simply say 'Father' and He takes you home.

The portrait of the caring protector

We must go back into the previous chapter to find the next feature recorded only by Luke. You have probably looked at it before and wondered about it. In 22:35, Jesus has warned Peter of the approaching danger and his certain defection, and He says to the disciples: 'When I sent you out without purse or bag or sandals on the Galilean mission—did you lack anything, were you short of anything?'

'Nothing,' they answered. 'All our needs were met. People welcomed us into their homes, folk provided shelter and food for us. We were lovingly and graciously received.'

He says to them 'It's going to be different from now on. Oh yes, there will be days when there'll be people will lovingly greet you and welcome you and care for you, but now if you have a purse you must take it with you because you are going into a society where people won't always want to give to you. Indeed, they'll want to take from you. Take a bag too, and if you don't have a sword then sell your cloak and buy one.'

It's an obviously vivid and arresting metaphor. The Lord Jesus couldn't tell them to love their enemies and then ask them to literally buy swords. It's a vivid arresting way of conveying a most important truth, like the Old Testament prophets did. If you want something to stay in people's minds, there's no point in giving some bland easily-forgettable statement. 'If your hand offends you, cut it off'—you don't mean that if you have a materialistic world view you should sever your hand at the wrist. 'If your eye offends you', if you're one of those people who have problems from looking at the wrong books or videos, 'pluck it out!'—but it doesn't mean you should literally do so. You know where your weak spot is. This is a metaphor. Jesus is saying, 'Look, you're going into a war situation. And what I want to say to you is that in one way or another you will need protection.' He is not urging them to purchase swords.

In fact it's obvious from the narrative, because actually they do have two swords. That was surprising, wasn't it? They must have feared that it was going to be dark and dangerous. They say to Him, 'We've got two.' And Jesus, when He says 'That is enough', doesn't mean that two would be adequate for the eleven them. Plainly they wouldn't. Jesus means, 'Enough of this! You haven't got the point. I don't want to carry on this conversation about fighting. You haven't grasped it. Perhaps one day you will.'

He didn't want them to use swords. He was appalled when one of those swords was shortly used to lacerate the face of the high priest's servant, because He said, 'Put that away' in Matthew's account. Those who take the sword will die by the sword.

So of course Jesus wasn't really expecting them to buy swords. What He was saying to them here was that they would need protection in the future. Oh the realism of it—they would need to stand by each other in trials and tribulations, they would need sensitive intercession because they were going into warfare, into the arena. Jesus was warning them, He was being their caring protector. He didn't want them to be taken by surprise, He loved them so much.

The portrait of the merciful healer

Now come to the fourth picture with me, and I think this is a picture of the most incomparable beauty. I find it almost difficult to talk about it. It's that terrible moment in the arrest when one of those who had heard all the teaching about loving your enemies and praying for those who despitefully use you reaches for his sword.

Doubtless it was done in fear, because it must have been

terrifying. The lantern was coming through the dark, Judas coming forward, kissing Jesus even passionately. The staves, the clashing, the swords and the soldiers. And this man lashes out at the first person he can see. The story is so important for all the four writers of the Gospels that they each tell us about it.

Mark provides the basic facts. Matthew provides us with the details of the conversation. John identifies both the victim and the offender, telling us that the victim's name was Malchus (I don't think there was any point in saying that, unless he'd become part of the Christian community); and he alone tells us who the offender was. It was, not surprisingly, Peter.

What does Luke tell us? Well, if we only had Matthew, Mark and John we'd have all wondered what happened to that desperate man's face. But Luke tells us that Jesus healed him. You'd expect a doctor to point that out, wouldn't you? Those lovely hands that throughout His whole ministry had been so kind, good, practical and helpful were going to be nailed to a cross. And the last thing He does with them is to touch the dreadful, desperate, bleeding face of this man.

Jesus is the one who comes to do things for people in mercy and love, even though they're enemies, even though they're rebels. He doesn't just heal and reach out in mercy to his friends. He does not only stand by His partners. No; in His great love He comes even to minister in mercy and grace, to people who've come to arrest Him and have set their faces against Him.

That's why in his second volume Luke is desperate to tell us a story about a rebel. He couldn't arrest Jesus because Jesus had ascended to the glory, but he was determined to arrest all His followers and put them in prison. Saul of Tarsus was actually engaged on that mission of destruction when Jesus the merciful healer came and met him, touched him and transformed him. What that must have meant to Luke's earliest readers, as they went out to face their enemies! It meant: Look, whatever you do, remember that Jesus can change them. He did something for that man.

The portrait of the loving friend

The fifth picture that Luke alone preserves for us is found in

22:61. All the Gospels tell us about Peter's denial of Jesus in the garden, how Peter let Jesus down. His courage failed, not his faith, but as we all know Peter went out and wept.

But Luke tells us why. It's not only because of what he said, but because of what he saw. He saw the face of Jesus (verse 61). Nobody else tells us that. Earlier (verse 56) we are told that a servant girl kept looking at him in the firelight. He must have felt desperately uncomfortable. It's the very same word that Luke uses when he's describing in chapter 4 Jesus preaching at the synagogue in Nazareth. The eyes of everybody were fixed on Him, they couldn't take their eyes off Him. Stared at in the same way by the servant girl he became more and more uncomfortable, until finally she recognised his face by the firelight and said, 'I know you.' And he said, 'Woman, I don't know Him.' What he didn't know was that Jesus was near enough to hear him, and had heard it.

Later he said it again to a man—'I do not know what you're talking about!' And the Lord turned and looked straight at Peter. It's a different verb. It's not the same as the girl's searching, accusing stare. It's only a loving glance. But searching glances can scan the very wounds that shame would hide.

The early Christians knew that. There would be days when they would let Jesus down. But what a wonderful thing to know, when He looked at them—yes, He would look at them—and they realised how awful it was, that He would not gloss over our sins and make excuses for them. They would never be healed like that. They would never be healed and forgiven unless they were brought out into the open. We need those searching eyes, those eyes like flame. That's why Peter went out and wept; it was seeing the face of Christ looking at him and right into him, and seeing as Jesus looked at him all those brash things that he'd said in moments of high but uncostly heroism.

The portrait of the reliable prophet

You must allow me just to say a word about another picture, in 23:27-31. It's the picture of Jesus talking to the woman. Here are the women surrounding the victims, as so often they did at crucifixions. But Simon of Cyrene has carried the *patibulum*, the big heavy cross bar, and there's something very significant about that: 'You've got to take your cross and follow Me.' But because the heavy weight of that crippling cross was off His shoulders for those moments, He could look up and see these women who were round about Him crying. And I want you to notice that even then He has a message.

He doesn't *only* love, it's not *only* by healing, it's not *just* by miracle, it's also by what He said. Try to trace the importance of what He says to them. He is saying something about Himself: 'Don't weep for Me.' You mustn't come to the cross with pity for Jesus. You must come to the cross with praise for Jesus. You come to the cross with pity for yourself.

It's sin that took Him there. He was obeying the Father's will, He was rejoicing in the love of the Father. He talked about Himself, He talked about themselves. 'Weep for yourselves.' He talked about the future and your children. He talked about the Bible, quoting from Hosea 10:8, and talked about how sin gets worse and worse (verse 31).

You can study two further pictures on your own. There's the invincible conqueror: Jesus heard one man declare Him to be a king when all others were ridiculing Him: 'Lord, remember me when You come to Your kingdom. They're all saying it in ridicule, but I believe it. You've done nothing amiss.' He is the invincible conqueror because He says on the cross that the cross is not the end, though all round Him believed it was. He was going to paradise, He was going to glory; and He was going to take this man, of all men, with Him—a rebel, a criminal, a brigand—this man who was coming to faith in Jesus.

And the last picture is of the trusting son: 'Father, into your hands I commit my spirit.'

4. The Glorified Son
(John 18:1–19:42)

We're going to think this morning about John's magnificent portrayal of the Lord Jesus as the glorified Son of God who comes to renew the confidence of all His people.

I have said already in these Bible Readings that the writers of the Gospels have different and distinctive emphases. That is certainly so with this beautiful Gospel of John. It is probably the last to be written, and is certainly different in structure and in style. If Matthew the tax collector, brought to personal faith in Jesus—but aware of the dangers of money—wants to expose the sin that made the cross necessary; if Mark the young man whose robe was snatched at the moment of the arrest wants to present to us the urgency of Christ's message of Christ and the importance of following Him; if Luke the doctor has his signature in the Gospels, concealed through some of the medical language which is found in the Gospel and in the Acts of the Apostles; then John likewise identifies himself, as the disciple whom Jesus loved.

He is not suggesting that others are not loved. It's just that he treasures the fact that Jesus loves him. It's possible to say 'I am so glad that Jesus loves me' without saying that He doesn't love other people too—it's just an expression of your overflowing gratitude. And if Mark hides himself in the dark corner of the picture by describing himself (as I believe he does) as that young man who failed in his following at that moment, then John hides himself too by referring to himself in this way. He's emphasising that the most important thing in the Christian life is to be loved by Jesus and to know that He loves you so much that He died for you on this cross.

John knows that it's going to be costly to follow Christ. To confess His deity was an offence, particularly in a Jewish world, and time and again in this Gospel the readers are confronted with the tension of confessing Christ as the matchless and unique Son of God when such an assertion was regarded by their Jewish neighbours and friends as nothing short of blasphemy. Furthermore, to say 'Jesus is Lord' was a dangerous confession in the first-century world. If the open confession of the deity of Christ was an offence to many Jewish people, the confession of the lordship of Christ was certainly an offence to Roman citizens, because Caesar was lord. So, religiously and politically, Christians were exposed to opposition.

As the century moved on, it was becoming increasingly dangerous in both these arenas to confess the uniqueness of Christ. And I believe that the Gospel of John is seeking, among other things, to provide for people who will find it tough to make confession of Christ, and to remind them of the great truths of the Christian gospel by which they are sustained.

If Matthew's Gospel points out that the gospel is for sinners, and Mark's Gospel calls you to heroism and courage in the way of the cross; and if Luke's Gospel is saying that you can only make that confession and go on in your walk with Christ if you keep looking to Jesus the sensitive inter-cessor, caring protector, merciful healer, loving friend and so on—then John's Gospel reflects upon the teaching in the other Gospels and on the great truths that are being trea-sured by the Christian community; supremely, on the prom-ised ministry of the Holy Spirit, a promise preserved by John: 'He will take the things that belong to Me, the things that are said about Me, the things that I did, the miracles I per-formed; and He will bring them to your remembrance, He will keep them green and fresh in your minds.' That's why we have these lovely Gospels.

Of course they're a testimony to the fact that people who

heard the beautiful things Jesus said and remembered the marvellous things He had done and kept on recalling them in their conversation. These things belonged to the very heart of their life; they were unforgettable. Before anybody set anything down in writing, what did they preach about? They preached about these stories. The Gospels preserve the exposition and proclamation of the Christian community through forty years or so. People had been eye-witnesses; they knew the reality and reliability of some of these great truths. And the Holy Spirit made sure that these events, sayings and miracles were preserved in Scripture.

So John of all the Gospel writers is perhaps the most aware of the wealth of material that might be included, and he knows he has to be selective. Luke says in his prologue that he knows others wrote down the gospel story. But John at the end of his Gospel (20:30) tells us that Jesus did many more things in the presence of His disciples that are not recorded in his book: 'I've selected the material, and these are written so that you might believe that Jesus is Christ the Son of God'—so that you might be able to make the same confession doubting Thomas made, who was not present at the Christian meeting when these things began to be talked about, but was brought to faith in Christ and commitment and confession of His lordship; who said in the presence of Jesus, 'My Lord and my God.' He thereby acknowledged the deity of Christ, though that would have been an offence to the non-Christian Jew. He acknowledged His lordship, which would have been such an irritation to the Roman who believed that Caesar was lord. These things are written so that we too might make that same confession and that then and now, people might like Thomas know the reality of commitment, of confession of Him.

'And that by believing, you might have life in His name'— that meant for them the great treasure of eternal life, because of the death of the Lord Jesus on the cross. He came into the world to die, He laid down His life that we might live. 'God so loved the world that he gave his one and only Son, that whoever believes in him shall not perish but have eternal life' (3:16).

Among John's contemporaries were those who rejoiced

that eternal life was their certain, present possession. But some would be called upon to pay the price in blood. They laid down their lives for the gospel, but they did so in the calm assurance that nobody could snatch life from them. They knew their lives were in the hands of the Good Shepherd who had given His life for the sheep, who said 'Nobody would be able to pluck them out of My Father's hand'; they knew that they were already enjoying eternal life, but that it was a life that could never be taken away. It destined them for heaven. If they made that great confession, 'My Lord and My God', then by believing they would have life, in that name: the Son of God, the Lord, Jesus who would save His people from their sins.

So what is happening in John's Passion narrative is that he is striving to impress upon the reader, as this marvellous Gospel draws to its close, some great Christian truths that can sustain believing men and women through dark days as well as through bright days. There are themes here that Christians need to store away in their spiritual memory, to make them—to change the imagery—the strong foundation upon which they stand.

Here are the great truths of what it means distinctively to be a believer in a world where it may be dangerous to be a Christian. It was certainly perilous in the communities that were strong in their Jewish allegiance as the century wore on; but by the beginning of the second century it was becoming impossible for an honest Christian to be present in a synagogue; the 'synagogue benedictions' required all present to call down a curse on the followers of the Nazarene. So it is especially significant that in chapter 18 at the beginning of this Passion narrative Jesus twice says 'Who are you looking for?' And his arresters twice say 'We are looking for Jesus of Nazareth.' It's the Nazarene! Some were reading this Gospel who knew how dangerous it was to say in the synagogue that you belonged to the Nazarene. It was dangerous too in the political arena, as we've seen.

How do people gain strength, courage and confidence? By the great truths of the gospel. I want to suggest to you that we find those truths in John 18 and 19. And, as I've said in the previous Bible Readings, there are distinctive elements in each of these Gospels. You will find twenty-five, perhaps thirty distinctive features in these two chapters that are not found in the other Gospels. I'm not going to look at them all this morning just as I didn't go through every one of Luke's distinctives yesterday; but I want us to look at some of them, because I believe they enshrine some of the most important truths for Christian believers not just in the first century but also in our own times.

And I believe they're especially relevant in a society like ours, attracted to pluralism—the view that all religions are equally valid. If you believe in Islam—well, it's your way of coming to God. If it's Hinduism, then that's your way. If it's Judaism, Shintoism, Confucianism—that's your way; whatever it may be. This Gospel is addressed to that kind of society, where there were competing religious as well as political allegiances in the first century.

So I want to suggest to you that in John's thinking the cross is, first of all,

The place of unique glory

John's most significant moment at the beginning of the Passion narrative comes in 18:4, and it's easily missed. Look at this detail that John alone preserves in the Gospel: a Saviour who marches out to meet those who come to arrest Him, knowing exactly what is going to happen to Him. 'Who is it you want?'

'We're after the Nazarene. Jesus of Nazareth, we've come to arrest Jesus of Nazareth.'

If we just look at it briefly, casually moving on to things we think of greater importance, we could easily miss this. It is the 'I am'. Three times in this narrative the words are used. And when Jesus said (verse 6) 'I am he', they drew back and fell to the ground—there's a detail that's not found in the other Gospels. There was something about Him saying that at that moment that totally overwhelmed them. They collapsed and fell to the ground. 'Who do you want?' Jesus asks them. Again, as they're collapsed on the floor, they reply, 'We want the Nazarene, we've come to arrest Jesus of Nazareth.'

'I tell you that I am He.'

It's a detail that's easily missed, but 'I am' is a great Old Testament title for God. It's two little words that are used in the Greek testament and the Septuagint (the Greek version of the Old Testament): *ego eimi*—'I am'—repeated for emphasis. It's in the continuous present tense: not 'I am the one who was', the God of the past, but the God of the past and the present and the future. 'I am'—the changeless one, the eternal one. It's the same title that the Lord Jesus applies to Himself in the 'I am' sayings in this Gospel—'I am the Bread of Life', 'I am the door of the sheep', 'I am the Good Shepherd', 'I am the true vine', 'I am the resurrection and the life'.

It first occurs in a most wonderful setting, in chapter 6 after the great miracle of the feeding of the multitude. He went up into the hills, because the crowd wanted to make Him king, and it wasn't the time for the declaration of His kingship. His kingship was going to be declared from a cross, not by an enthusiastic crowd at a great banquet. So Jesus climbed up into the hills, but His disciples got into a boat. There was a storm, and the waves tossed the boat backwards and forwards and they were terrified. They were even more fearful when they saw the Lord Jesus walking to them on the water. He said to them, 'It is I; don't be afraid' (6:20). It's *ego eimi* again—'I am'; it is God present in the person of His unique Son. They need not fear.

This moment recalls the great moments of Hebrew history, and one of the great titles of God in the Old Testament. It's the moment when Moses, isolated and bewildered in the Desert of Midian, sees a bush flaming with fire. He's amazed; the bush is not consumed. It is impossible, this inextinguishable fire. He draws near and he's in the presence of God who is calling him to an extremely difficult task. He too is going to be in an alien situation, he's being sent back into a dangerous arena. But as He commissions him to his task God says, 'When they ask you who has sent you you must say "I am has sent you"'—the changeless, never failing, eternal, ever sufficient God who will always be by your side' (cf. Exodus 3).

So Jesus' declaration at the moment of His arrest is a most significant point in the narrative. Like many students of the New Testament I believe that that's why His accusers fell back. It was the moment of overwhelming unique glory, just as when the revelation of God was seen in Old Testament times and people fell to the ground. When Ezekiel had that overwhelming vision of God, in exile, he fell to the ground. It came too to Daniel and overwhelmed him (Daniel 10:9). It came to John, when he saw the majestic Son of God on Patmos: 'When I saw him, I fell at his feet as though dead' (Rev. 1:17). Then, the Lord Jesus was taking the titles that belonged to God in the Old Testament: 'I am the First and the Last and the Living One, the Never-failing One, the I am.' And that's what is being said right at the beginning of this Passion narrative. Jesus is God manifest in the flesh, God's unique and only Son—'I am he'. That's why they fell to the ground.

And Christian believers needed that assurance that the Lord Jesus was not simply an attractive prophet, an outstanding miracle-worker, a gifted healer, a dependable friend. He is God manifest in the flesh. This Gospel ends in this way because it began in that way. 'In the beginning was the Word, and the Word was with God, and the Word was God... And the Word was made flesh, and dwelt among us, (and we beheld his glory, the glory as of the only begotten of the Father,) full of grace and truth' (1:1,14 AV). And that's why, right at the end, in this most unexpected place when they're coming with lanterns and torches and staves to arrest Him— in the dark and dangerous hour Jesus says, 'I am'. God was present among them in His Son. And Christian believers who would find life tough and difficult in the hazardous first-century world must remember that they had committed their lives to Christ, the matchless Son of God who would never have failed them.

The place of eternal security

Look at another detail that only John preserves, in 18:8. The Lord Jesus had walked out to meet His accusers, He knew that they were coming for Him. But at that moment He was concerned about the rather frail band of brothers behind Him—those, as we were thinking yesterday, who had stood by Him in His trials and testings. But most of whom would leave Him in a few hours.

In the hour of extreme danger He was concerned for their safety, that they shouldn't be arrested. And so He stands at that point between the powers that would arrest and the little group that was in danger. He interposes Himself, and He says, 'Let these men go. You've come to arrest Me; but don't put their lives in danger.'

In the other Gospels you can see the others hurriedly scurrying away, but John has recalled the detail that's been attested by eyewitnesses—that they didn't just scurry off; Jesus spoke on their behalf to those that would arrest them. He became in that moment a substitute between them and impending danger, and He protected them. He was the Good Shepherd who was giving His life for the sheep, and He promised them protection. He told them in this very Gospel that there would be dangers, that their lives would be in peril (15:18): 'If they persecuted Me they will certainly persecute you.' He is saying that if He protects them in that moment He knows that they will still in future moments be exposed to extreme danger. But here and now, He is saying to them, 'I am with you to protect you.' He spoke to the accusers so that the word might be fulfilled: 'I have lost none of those you gave me'—a reference back to the high-priestly prayer in the previous chapter.

We thought about that prayer yesterday, when we saw Him kneeling in the garden in Luke's dramatic picture of Gethsemane. John fills it out in greater detail. He's aware of the fact that Christ prayed for those who were in danger— 'While I was with them,' Jesus said as He prayed to His Father, 'I protected them, I kept them while they were with Me, I was with them and kept them safe by that name that you gave Me. But I beg you Father to protect them, to be alongside them, so that no one will pluck them out of the Father's hand' (cf. 17:12)

The cross in John is the place of eternal security, it is to know that the Lord Jesus is speaking for you and you are in His strong and mighty hands. Nothing is happening by accident. In this Gospel, Jesus knows exactly what is going to happen.

That theme recurs throughout this Gospel. Jesus knew in chapter 1 all about Nathaniel, while he was still under the fig tree. 'He knew what was in a man' (2:25). He knew all about the immoral life of the woman at the well in chapter 4: she said, 'You must be a prophet to be able to read that and know what's going on in my secretive life.' He knew at the beginning of chapter 6 exactly what He was going to do when the multitude came before Him hungry and a long way from home—He said to Philip, 'Where can we get bread to give enough for these people to eat?', but He was only testing him, He knew what He was going to do. At the end of the miracle, when they wanted to make Him king, He was aware of what they were thinking.

He knows what's happening. And this Gospel tells us, nothing is beyond the range of His knowledge and power and what He knows about Himself. He knows about us and sometimes will stand between us and the encroaching danger, protecting us, giving us that security that He's promised— 'Nobody will be able snatch them out of the Father's hand.' And if some of the readers of this Gospel, and some of the great people who followed Him through Christian history had not been spared, just as He was not spared, from the shedding of blood, then they were with Him safe for ever. He protected them for eternity. It was only for a little while that life was snatched away. They entered into His glory, they were with Him for ever.

The place of renewed confidence

Confidence in what? Confidence in the word of Christ and the word of God. He said, 'You've come to arrest me; be content with that, let these men go.' He said this (verse 9) 'so that the words he had spoken would be fulfilled: "I have not lost one of those you gave me." ' Later, in verse 32, the Jews said to Pilate 'We have no right to execute anyone': 'This happened so that the words Jesus had spoken indicating the kind of death he was going to die would be fulfilled.'

He had said throughout His ministry that He was going to die. So what this is saying is that the word of Jesus will come true; it's a reliable word. And the word must be fulfilled. He had to die. But not as the Jews might have wished to execute Him by stoning on a charge of blasphemy, had they been able. He knew He had to die upon a cross, He had to be lifted up as the serpent was lifted up in the wilderness; He had to be that grain of wheat that would fall into the ground and die.

These first-century believers had many claims upon their allegiance. Many were brought to times of testing and needed to have renewed confidence in the word of Christ in verse 18 and the word of God in verse 19. Look into chapter 19: John keeps reiterating this great truth: You can trust the word that has been given. If God has said it, if Christ has said it, it is true. You can depend upon it.

Look at 19:24. The soldiers were deciding what to do about their perks—the garments they could claim from any crucified victim. There are five garments and only four soldiers; there's one left over. 'Don't tear it!' somebody says. 'Let's cast lots to see who'll get it.' They had no idea that they were fulfilling the Scripture. God had already said it through the Psalmist in Psalm 22, the very psalm Jesus had treasured in His mind when He was on that cross—'They divide my garments among them and cast lots for my clothing' (Psalm 22:18). Humanly speaking it was totally impossible for people to fulfil that prophecy in that precise way at that precise moment—unless God planned it. And what it was saying to Christian people was, Look: if God has said these great truths in His word in the Old Testament, and if Christ has said these great things that will be treasured in what is to be the New Testament, you can depend with renewed confidence upon the word that will fit you for the future.

In 19:28 He calls out 'I am thirsty'; it is so that the Scripture will be fulfilled, verse 15 of that same psalm. Look down the chapter to verse 36, the smitten side of the Lord Jesus: 'These things happened so that the Scripture would be fulfilled: "Not one of his bones will be broken," and, as another Scripture says, "They will look on the one they have pierced." '

It's the story in the Pentateuch of the Passover lamb. It's the story in those marvellous prophetic words of Zechariah 12. You can depend upon the words that Jesus has said. And people stand firm in times of testing and pressure and adversity, if they know the word and trust it.

The place of obedient surrender

Go back, if you will, to 18:11. It's the awful moment the other writers of the Gospels have recorded so faithfully in their pages, when the peace lover, the peace giver, the peace bringer was arrested, the Lord Jesus who made peace by the blood of His cross. At that moment those who were closest to Him were those who had heard His teaching about peace, loving your enemies and turning the other cheek. One of them, the impetuous Peter, took his sword and struck the high priest's servant Malchus. And in verse 11 Jesus speaks to Peter. 'Put your sword away! Look, this is not the time for aggression but submission. Shall I not drink the cup the Father has given Me? This is not a time for wielding swords, but for drinking the cup.'

The cup of suffering; but I believe—as readers of this Gospel would have believed who were lovers of the Old Testament—that it is also the cup of wrath. If you read the great prophetic messages of Isaiah, Jeremiah and Ezekiel for example, you will find they all preserve the language and imagery of the cup of God's wrath. The cup was not only of an atrocious and ghastly physical death, the cup from which He had asked to be spared; Jesus was drinking to the dregs the cup of the wrath of God. 'In my place condemned He stood, sealed my pardon with His blood, hallelujah! what a Saviour.'

'My friends,' He said, 'the cup which the Father has given Me, shall I not drink it?' Is it not beautiful that what the other Gospels keep for the Gethsemane narrative, John brings into the heart of the Passion narrative at the moment of arrest? Actually, he often does that. With his supreme and superbly meditative style he says to us, in all sorts of different contexts, that what Jesus did at specific precise occasions He also repeated at other times through His life.

John doesn't actually have a Gethsemane passage as such. He incorporates it into the ministry of Jesus at more than one place. In 12:27, in the streets in Jerusalem: 'Now my heart is troubled, and what shall I say? "Father, save me from this hour"?' It's the very theme of the Gethsemane story. But it's all anticipated by John. In other words, that testing didn't come to Jesus just once. 'No, it was for this very reason I came to this hour. Father, glorify your name!' Your will be done.

Similarly John doesn't have a baptism-of-Jesus narrative as such. John the Baptist describes it (1:32-34), but there isn't an actual narrative. But there are moments through the Gospel when all that it means is made public: the Sonship of Christ, the uniqueness of the Lord Jesus, demonstrated to everybody, not just to a group of people who happened to be there at the River Jordan.

The temptation narrative isn't found in John's Gospel as it's found in the other three Gospels as a narrative at the beginning of the story. Why? Well because it keeps happening all through the Gospel. In chapter 4, He is even tempted even by His disciples. 'Master' they keep saying to Him, 'Come on.' They keep asking Him, 'Eat, we've been for these provisions, come and eat now.' He says there's something now more important than eating; man shall not live by bread only. 'Why, there's a harvest to be reaped, there's all these Samaritans coming now through the fields, they need to know about the message just as this woman has heard about the life-giving purifying waters within.' In chapter 6 He's offered the kingdom, just as in the temptation narratives He was offered all the kingdoms of the world in a moment of time. 'Get behind Me Satan'—and Satan is coming now in the guise of the crowd. It's not just once that temptation comes.

In chapter 7 it's the brothers of Jesus who are wearing the tempter's robe. 'If You want to be acclaimed You've got to go public, You must show Yourself in Jerusalem. Go to the place where the action is.' It's another form of the temptation. Jesus says 'No, I'm not going at this moment, I'm going when the Father wants it.' It's like the third temptation, 'Leap from the temple, perform a sign.' That's what His brothers were saying in chapter 7, wasn't it? 'You must go public.' No, John makes sure that we see the temptations in the life of Christ throughout His ministry and not just at specific moments.

There's no Lord's Table scene, no Passover feast scene in John—because He is the true vine, the one who has shed His precious blood. It's in the teaching of the Gospel. And this is saying that the cross is the place of obedient surrender, where the Lord Jesus yields Himself fully and completely to the will of the Father, and does for us what we cannot possibly do for ourselves—He obtains our eternal salvation.

But He is offering stark alternatives to Peter. It's in this very Gospel that Peter is told he must walk the way of martyrdom—you remember the story in 21:17-19. The cross in John is the place of obedient surrender. That's so for us. John is saying that there's no place in the Christian life for handling the things the way the world handles its troubles and difficulties and crises. The world's way is the way of the sword—hit back! That was Peter's way. But the way of Christ is the way of the cup, it's the way of submission, of surrender, of obedience. It's the costly way.

The place of costly substitution

Verses 12-18 of chapter 18 are a small historical detail. They are all that has been preserved. Yet John makes the point to remind his readers of something he's said earlier.

Verse 14, 'Caiaphas was the one who had advised the Jews that it would be good if one man died for the people.' It's characteristic of John's Gospel that people often say and do things without realising the eternal significance of what they're saying and doing. And this reminds the reader to look back, as it were, at what is preserved for us in 11:49-52, where Caiaphas said those words to the people. 'He did not say this on his own'—he didn't know what he was saying—but he was prophesying the death of Jesus for the Jewish nation to bring together and unify the scattered children of God. 'So from that day on they plotted to take his life.'

Costly substitution. There would be believers who would die because they loved Jesus. When, as many of them were, they were opposed by Jewish neighbours who were determined to hunt them down and Roman officials and magistrates who were to lead some of them to execution, they all knew only too well that though they might give their lives because they loved Jesus, they were not giving their lives to save themselves. The life had already been given. They knew they were making their surrender and walking the way of suffering because they wanted to show that they belonged to

Christ, that they were with Him for ever. But they knew that
there was a uniqueness about that death. He had died once
and for all. He died not only for the Jewish nation but for all
people He died as a substitute, He died in their place. 'In my
place, condemned He stood.'

That was one of the great truths of the Gospel that these
early Christian believers had to go out to proclaim to their
neighbours, because they were surrounded all the time by
people who said in various ways that salvation, which they
didn't deny as a possibility—a higher kind of life, a better
quality of life—had to be gained by oneself. You had to do it
yourself: some extra work to do, some extra knowledge to
acquire, some way of life to attain to. And the readers of this
Gospel were perceptive enough to understand that John is
saying that what Jesus did for them on the cross was—to use
his majestic language—a finished work. You cannot add to
it.

It was an essential truth for the first-century Christian
community and it still is for us. What is most offensive about
the gospel to most of your neighbours is that they can't do
anything to earn it. They don't mind it becoming a Christian
as long as they can do their little bit. If you go on a house-to-
house evangelistic visitation, then however sensitively you
talk about Jesus sooner or later somebody will respond,
'Well—thank you very much, but you know I really believe
that you've got be kind to your neighbours and lead a good
life, and I try to do my best.' It's the desire to earn our own
salvation.

That's why at the heart of the Passion narrative we read 'It
will be good if one man died for the people.' The cross is the
place of costly substitution.

The place of bold confession

From 18:15 onwards John does a remarkable thing. He tells
how Peter gained admission into the high priest's garden, and
he interrupts the story of the interrogation of Jesus to tell the
story of the interrogation of Peter.

Peter's gained admission and a girl on duty says, 'You're
not one of this man's disciples, are you?'

'I am not.'

Jesus has said, 'I am'. Peter says, 'I am not'. As we have seen, it's a question of how and how not to make your confession of faith.

Immediately (verse 19) this interrogation is interrupted with the interrogation of Jesus. 'Meanwhile the high priest questioned Jesus about his disciples'—about people like Peter who was being interrogated possibly at that very moment—'and his teaching.'

'I have spoken openly to the world,' Jesus replied. Peter, secretive in the corner of the garden, is terrified that this girl will see his face in the firelight. 'I always taught in synagogues or at the temple, where all the Jews come together. I said nothing in secret.' It's a call for bold confession, not to do what Peter did, to skulk away in the corner like a coward in secret but to stand up—'Stand up for Jesus, you soldiers of the cross. Lift high His royal banner, it must not suffer loss.'

All of us, if we are at all sensitive, are deeply conscious of the awful fact that our Christian life is littered with examples of times when we might have said a word for Jesus. But we were just a little afraid, somewhat preoccupied, rather busy with something else; or we couldn't find the right word, we didn't think it was the best opportunity.

But here is a call to bold confession. And throughout Christian history, thank God, there are people who are ready to say openly to the world that they belong to Christ, to say not 'I am not', but, as Jesus said, 'I am'.

The place of assured victory

As you read this narrative one thing cannot fail to strike you; the repeated assertion that Jesus is king. It's John's favourite theme. You can explore at your leisure John's assertion of the kingship of Christ, that in this Gospel, the Lord Jesus reigns as king from the tree. He rules from the cross. He's in control of His destiny. It's these poor people, on the contrary, who are being pushed around, pressurised and manipulated.

Like poor Pilate, scurrying, wanting to insist that Jesus is innocent, three times saying in chapters 18 and 19, 'I can't find any basis of a charge in Him. I find no basis for a charge in Him.' He doesn't know that the one he addresses as king,

and interrogates about His kingship and His kingly rule, and
announces as 'king' as he leads Him out, actually *is* king. But
Christians who first read this Gospel knew the reality and
truth of that. That confession of the kingship of Christ had
been made in the very opening passages of this Gospel. A
cynic, Nathaniel demanded 'Can any good thing come out of
Nazareth?'; he was dismissive of the Nazarene. But at the
end of the Gospel, Jesus is the king, ruling and reigning from
the tree.

Pilate doesn't really know what he's doing. He's making
this title, having it inscribed—The Nazarene, the king, the
despised one, the one who's come from a town of nothing
and nobodies, Jesus of Nazareth, the King of the Jews. The
Jewish people are offended. 'Write that He *said* He was the
king. It's not a fact, it's just His assertion.' But Pilate refused.
It's in Hebrew, Greek and Latin. The world will read it and
understand it. The world may look on in scorn, because how
can you believe it? The king on a cross! Kings go to their
thrones and trample people down. But this king reigns from
the cross. And in his magnificent Book of the Revelation,
John tells us that this king is King of kings and Lord of lords.

It was in written in Hebrew, but the Jews couldn't believe
that a crucified man could possibly be king; 'Cursed is everyone who hangs on a tree' (Gal. 3:13)—He must be a blas-
phemer.

It was written in Greek, but the Greeks said that God
couldn't possibly die. God could scarcely feel anything, He
couldn't go through the experience of death. A dying God
was a contradiction in terms to the Greeks.

It was written in Latin, but the Romans couldn't believe it.
God—a king, crucified? Why, you couldn't even crucify a
Roman citizen. It was illegal to do so. It was the death for a
common criminal. But Jesus is the king ruling from the tree
in the place of assured victory.

The place of unfailing love

Isn't it beautiful in chapter 19 that, while the soldiers are
thinking about what they can get from this crucifixion scene,
casting lots for the garment, the Lord Jesus is considering
what's going to happen to His dear mother. 'Having loved his

own...he loved them to the end' (13:1, AV). It's only John who preserves that lovely detail for us, that He was concerned about her. If you really love somebody you are more concerned about what is going to happen to them than about yourself.

John, like Luke, has time and again through his Gospel said lovely things about women and given them such prominence in his narrative. Look at the women in these Gospels some time. They're all central people, they're not marginal people. It's saying something very profound about equality to the male-dominated first-century world. 'Look after this dear mother of mine, will you, John?'

The cross is the place of unfailing love even at the end. Jesus isn't thinking about Himself. He's not thinking about things, as the soldiers were. He was thinking about people. They were thinking about the present, and the robe they would get. He was thinking about the future, what would happen to His mother when He'd gone. The Gospel of John presents the cross as the place of unfailing love.

And finally, and perhaps most beautifully, the cross is,

The place of complete pardon

'It is finished!' Did you know, it's said twice, in 19:28 and 30. 'Later, knowing that all was now completed'—it's the same word in Greek as in 'It is finished', *teleo*. It's done! The work is finished, complete! He'd fully done the will of the Father. All that was necessary for your salvation and mine was accomplished, knowing that all was now complete. There's nothing more that you can do. On the basis of that finished work of the Lord Jesus Christ, your salvation is secure for ever. Oh, God be praised, that the cross in John is the place of complete pardon!

Is there someone here with a haunting sense of guilt from which you're still not free? Perhaps you feel you've failed like the disciples did. These are not perfect people portrayed in these Gospels, not one of them. There's only one who was pure and spotless and undefiled and perfect, and that's the Saviour who died for them and bore their sin in His own body on that tree, who drank that cup of suffering for them.

You can be forgiven. Jesus said, 'It is finished.' There's

nothing you can do, there's no extra little bit of remorse that He requires of you. If you will just look to Him in penitence and tell that you're deeply sorry, that you repent, you can be forgiven.

Now this is where the Passion narratives end, with the love and devotion of those who carried Him to His grave (so He wasn't buried as a common criminal as they thought He might be). John goes on to tell the story of the Resurrection: that's another story and I must leave it to someone else to expound it. But thank God for the reality of it! Jesus is risen. And these people who witnessed these scenes and hurried away from them in fear and buried themselves in safe places in Jerusalem, could say within just a day or two, 'The Lord is risen indeed!' Thanks be to God.

THE ADDRESSES

'I SAW THE LORD'

by Mr Chua Wee Hian

Isaiah 6

In a few days time you'll be home among friends. They'll ask, 'How was Keswick?' And you might say: 'The singing was fantastic...the messages were challenging and stirring...I enjoyed great fellowship.' They might nod in approval, and then someone might say, 'Let's have lunch', or 'Let's continue with the Sunday School teachers' meeting'. But if you were asked what happened at Keswick 1992 and you said, 'I saw the Lord, the Lord met with me'—there might be a startled silence! And then you'd have to explain.

Over 2,700 years ago the prophet Isaiah declared 'I saw the Lord...My eyes have seen the King, the Lord Almighty.' And that vision, that glimpse of God transformed him and changed his entire ministry. We've come to Keswick neither for holy huddle nor spiritual picnic. We've come here primarily to meet with the living God.

Chapter 6 begins with those dramatic words, 'In the year that King Uzziah died, I saw the Lord seated on a throne, high and exalted, and the train of his robe filled the temple.' It was 740 BC, a critical period in the history of the nation of Judah. King Uzziah had reigned for fifty-two years; now he was dead. Isaiah was wondering: would the new king follow Yahweh, or would he simply compromise his faith? Would the nation of Judah survive, especially with the emergence of the super-power Assyria? Isaiah, God's messenger, was perplexed, confused—even fearful; until he met with the living God.

Tonight we are going to look at the transforming vision of the prophet Isaiah. I want to suggest to you that there are three gazes in three different directions.

The upward gaze

First of all, the upward gaze. 'I saw the Lord seated on a throne high and exalted...My eyes have seen the King, the Lord Almighty.' As he gazed upwards the first thing Isaiah saw was this:

God is sovereign (verse 1)

The throne of Judah might be empty, but the throne of heaven is always occupied. God is King. No abdication or coup can topple Him. He reigns for ever and ever. Hallelujah! My eyes have seen the King.

At one time many preachers and politicians were saying, 'Look at the world. The red flag is flying in so many countries the whole earth will soon be red.' The hammer pounded, the sickle scythed and much of humanity came under the Marxist rule. But look what happened in recent times. We've seen the Berlin wall crumbling, we've seen the empire of Marxism being dismantled. God is in control. Some years ago Nikita Khrushchev, the Premier of the Soviet Union said 'We'll bury you. Marxism will march on, and nobody can stop this tide.' But look what's happened today. God is on the throne.

In 1969 I was a member of a group of committee members of the International Fellowship of Evangelical Students meeting in Singapore. We received a letter from an English student who was studying in Warsaw. He suggested that we should start work among students in the Eastern bloc. We had a very full agenda; it was at the height of the Cold War. It would have been easy to dismiss the letter. But we prayed. To my astonishment, everyone said 'Yes, let's consider this request.' We wrote back and asked him if he had anyone in mind for the job of unofficial travelling secretary in Eastern Europe. He had the audacity to write back and say 'Try me.' So we tried him. In God's sovereignty this man fell in love—I hope that we believe that truly falling in love is a sovereign act of God!—with a Hungarian student and they were married. That gave them the perfect cover; like Aquila and Priscilla in the New Testament they were able to visit student groups all over Eastern Europe. Later when there was freedom to express the Christian faith and message, student work in countries like Poland, Hungary and Czechoslovakia took off—because we recognised that God was sovereign. We did not dismiss that letter. We acted, we prayed and we've seen God working in all those countries, raising up strong evangelical student work.

The story of the church in China again tells us of God's sovereignty. At one time most Chinese Christians were located in the coastal cities. That was why men like Hudson Taylor formed the China Inland Mission to take the gospel to inland China. When the Marxists took over in 1949 many Christians were sent to the hinterland of China where they often had to share their faith in rather strange circumstances; and wherever Chinese Christians went they tried to start house churches. In 1951 there were only one million protestant Christians in China. Some of us knew there was severe persecution; as a result many backslid. Some gave up their faith. Would the church in China continue? But when we saw that God is sovereign, we found there was another story of the church in China.

For example, there was a house church to which, one Sunday during the cultural revolution in the mid-1960s, the Red Guards and the police came to arrest the Christians. Of course they went for the preacher first. Before they could reach him, the owner of the house said 'Don't touch him. It's my house. Arrest me.' Then the man who was leading the music said 'No! I was the man responsible for the singing and all the noise. Arrest me.' And someone else said 'No, I play the accordion and contribute to all this noise, you'd better put me in prison.' The puzzled police and Red Guards did not quite know what to do. In the end they arrested over sixty believers and clapped them in the local prison. But when they got in, guess what they did? They sang, they worshipped, they testified and many of the prisoners—many of them political prisoners—were converted. The authorities didn't know what to do; they had a meeting and concluded: 'Those

Christians are more dangerous in prison than outside! Let's release them.' That story could be multiplied in different parts of China. God is sovereign.

In 1978-9 when we were able to piece together developments in the church of China we discovered that there are more than fifty million believers there. Without props, missionaries and resources the church not only survived, it grew. Why? Because Christians had faith in a sovereign mighty God.

We need that vision of God, the King, the Lord of Hosts. Then we can work in advance with Him. Some of us are so worried about the political future of Europe and the world. Who is going to control the destiny of mankind? Will it be Brussels, Bonn, Beijing? Will it be the White House or Whitehall? My friends, the answer is—the throne room of Heaven. God is there and He is king. We need to look up, to remember that He is the sovereign Lord.

I was once in one of Billy Graham's student meetings. He told us of an encounter in the White House. A group of senators were discussing various mindsets towards the world, especially politics and leadership. They asked Billy, 'Billy, should we be pessimists or optimists when it comes to politics?' He told them 'I've read my Bible from cover to cover, from Genesis to Revelation. And I know one thing, God is going to win in the end. He is Lord, He is king.' You and I must have that unshakable confidence in the Lord God Almighty. So as Isaiah looked up and as we gaze up we see the Lord seated on His throne. He is sovereign.

God is holy (verse 2-4)

The seraphs are the burning fiery messengers; 'seraph' literally means 'burning one'. These fiery angelic beings, who stood and ministered in the presence of God, had to cover their faces, such was the awesome purity of God. Their song was 'Holy, holy, holy is the Lord Almighty; the whole earth is full of your glory.' That's the anthem of heaven. They celebrate the holiness of God. This theme song is repeated again in the Book of Revelation. John saw heaven open, and when he heard angelic beings singing it was the same song. So, brothers and sisters, let's make sure we know it!

When I was in theological college I once discussed a rather

acute theological problem with my Welsh room-mate: 'What language shall we use in heaven?' He assured me it would be Welsh. I made my claims for Chinese! We may not know the language of heaven, but we know one of the theme-songs of heaven. The holiness of the Lord of Hosts.

Isaiah as he looked up saw the holiness of God. Holiness is His primary attribute. In the Old Testament the word 'the Holy One' or 'the Holy One of Israel' occurs fifty times (for example, look at Isaiah 57:15). God's name and character are holy. That means He is wholly other, the transcendent God, the God of all glory and majesty.

As these angelic beings sang that song of holiness, what happened? 'The doorposts and the thresholds shook and the temple was filled with smoke' (verse 4).

You may recall another incident. After Solomon had prayed his great prayer of dedication at the consecration of the first temple, the glory of the Lord filled the temple. We're told that even the priests couldn't enter, such was the awe-some presence of God. 'Our God is like a consuming fire,' says the writer to the Hebrews. And whenever men and women saw God in His glory, when they encountered Him as the Holy God, they trembled at His presence.

Moses was looking after his sheep in Midian. Then came the burning bush where God revealed Himself to Moses. The first thing He said to him was, 'Take off your sandals, for the place where you are standing is holy ground' (Exod. 3:5). Moses had to learn to revere and worship God. Someone has speculated that if you and I had an encounter with God at the burning bush, we would not take off our shoes but say, 'Hold on there, God ! Let me get my camcorder.' We have no sense of who God is. We should bow in prostration, because the God we worship and meet is the living God. Until we see Him on His throne, until we understand and appreciate the holiness of God, at best our vision of God is warped and distorted.

As Karl Barth once put it, 'Let God be God.' God is sovereign and God is holy: our response should be like that of the hymn writer F. W. Faber:

My God, how wonderful Thou art,
    Thy Majesty how bright,

How beautiful Thy mercy-seat
   In depths of burning light!

How wonderful, how beautiful,
   The sight of Thee must be,
Thine endless wisdom, boundless power
   And awful purity!

The inward gaze

In the light of God's majesty and blazing holiness, Isaiah experienced something dramatic. He saw himself as God perceived him.

Remember, Isaiah was a royal prophet. He moved in and out of the court, a highly respected spokesman of God. If you look at Isaiah 5 you will see that he has already pronounced six woes on the people. Look at 5:8—'Woe to you who add house to house and join field to field'—he was lambasting the materialist. Verse 11—'Woe to those who rise early in the morning'—he's not against having a quiet-time early in the morning; he is opposing those who run after drink in the morning and 'stay up late at night till they are inflamed with wine'. Woe to the drunkards. Verse 18—'Woe to those who draw sin along with cords of deceit, and wickedness as with cart ropes'—these were evil-doers. Verse 20—'Woe to those who call evil good and good evil, who put darkness for light and light for darkness, who put bitter for sweet and sweet for bitter'—people whose values are upside down; woe to them, let them be anathema. Verse 21—'Woe to those who are wise in their own eyes and clever in their own sight.' Here are the boastful, the braggarts, the arrogant, the know-alls, wise in their own eyes and clever in their own sight. They also received the prophet's condemnation. And the sixth woe is again at those who are morally corrupt and champions at drinking wine: verse 22—'Woe to those who are heroes at drinking wine and champions at mixing drinks, who acquit the guilty for a bribe, but deny justice to the innocent.'

But when we turn to Isaiah 6:5 we discover that the seventh woe was pronounced on himself. ' "Woe to me!" I cried. "I am ruined! For I am a man of unclean lips, and I live among a people of unclean lips, and my eyes have seen the King, the Lord Almighty." ' When Isaiah looked up and saw the holiness of God he also saw his own impurity, his foul filthiness. And he cried up to God for mercy: 'My lips are unclean.'

We don't know whether our room is dusty or untidy until light shines in. Then we notice the dust and dirt. In the same way, only when the laser beam of God's holiness strikes into our hearts and shows our true colours will we realise how sinful and wretched we are. Every genuine encounter with God must lead us to repent, to acknowledge our sin; to feel a sense of revulsion against our sin and shortcoming. We are judged, we are exposed—no excuses.

Holiness is sadly a neglected priority in today's church. We place so much more emphasis on happiness. At Keswick we call men and women to holy living—yet it's not a party-line holiness. God forbid that there should be 'Keswick holiness'! We should call men and women to *biblical* holiness, to what God has said: 'Be holy because I am holy.' It's a command given by the Lord in both Old and the New Testaments.

What is evangelical piety or holiness like today? I want to suggest that there is in many parts of the evangelical church a self-centred godliness, a piety that stresses self-fulfilment—how God can meet my need, how God can satisfy my desires, how God can please me; instead of how I can please the living God. We just want to feel good, we're not concerned with God's honour, God's glory or God's holiness. Today's piety is self-absorption, it's not God-centred. Like Narcissus we look at our own reflection, we glory in our own image, we do not give praise and glory to God; we are self-centred and we wish that God would bless us and prosper us.

But biblical holiness means godliness. And true godliness is always rooted in God-centredness. Be Holy: Why? Because *I the Lord* am holy. Today in many of our churches we have inverted the true spiritual values. We rate skills over sanctity, dynamism over deep devotion, programmes over prayer. We do not take time to be holy. Holiness has a very low priority in our church teaching and activity. One of the greatest pastors in this land was Robert Murray McCheyne of St Peter's Church, Dundee. Once he presented his congregation with this incomplete phrase and asked each believer to

supply an ending: 'The greatest need of my church is...'
What would you have written? More resources? Greater man
power? More funds to carry on activities? A new building, a
huge team of staff? But the amazing answer which Robert
Murray McCheyne gave was this: 'The greatest need of my
church is my personal holiness.' It's only when men and
women are truly godly, holy in God's sight, when they hate
sin and love good, the truth and the Lord Himself, that God
can use them.

On another occasion Robert Murray McCheyne wrote
movingly to a young missionary who'd just been commissioned for missionary work:

> Do not forget the culture of the inner man; I mean, of the heart.
> How diligently the cavalry officer keeps his sabre clean and
> sharp! Every stain he rubs off with the greatest care. Remember
> you are God's sword, His instrument. It is not great talents God
> blesses, so much as great likeness to Jesus.

The holy minister is an aweful weapon in the hand of God.
To be holy means we hate sin, we agree with God's verdict on
sin and we long for increasing likeness to Jesus Himself. And
the danger today, dear friends, is this—we do not call sin,
sin. We're affected by the relativism of our age.

Recently in some evangelical papers some leaders of our
evangelical churches have aid we shouldn't condemn those
who live together unmarried. We should try to understand
them, to come to terms with their economic, social positions.
Yes—we must understand and love sinners; but we must tell
them God's way. We cannot compromise God's holiness. Sin
must be named as sin. We may not like the old-fashioned
word 'fornication', but it's still a sin against the holy God. We
cannot dilute or lower God's standard. When Joseph was
tempted and enticed by Lady Potiphar, what was his
response? He could easily have embarked upon an indecent
relationship. But Joseph said 'How could I do such a wicked
thing and sin against God?' He had a high and lofty view of
God, His holiness and His righteousness.

What are we debating in our evangelical churches today?
'Where can we draw a line that's acceptable to evangelical
theologians where ethics is concerned?'—'How far', say the

young people, 'can I go without offending God?' This is casuistry, not biblical ethics.

Isaiah was overwhelmed by God's righteousness, majesty and holiness. He began to cry out in despair, 'Woe is me! I am ruined, I am undone!' When somebody can say that, God steps in. That's the first step in becoming a man or woman of God. And what happened? In verse 6 we see what the seraph did. It's a significant act. Why? Because the live coal was taken from the altar. The whole altar reeked with the blood of animals. In the Old Testament as well as the New, there's one principal of forgiveness: without the shedding of blood there is no forgiveness of sin. The only way in which sins can be atoned for is by blood—and in the case of men and women today, only through the shed blood of the Lord Jesus Christ.

So the live coal had tremendous significance. It was taken from the altar where the sacrifice of atonement was made. And we see this reassuring word that the angel gave to Isaiah: 'This has touched your lips; your guilt is taken away and your sin atoned for.' I remember a young lad once asking me after he'd been to Sunday School, 'What is it that God cannot see?' I said 'I give up,' because I thought God could see everything. And he said 'God cannot see my sins when they are covered in Jesus' blood.' Isn't that a beautiful answer? Sin had been atoned for. The Hebrew word used here, *kippur*, means covered up, atoned for.

Brothers and sisters, the devil's ploy is this. He wants to accuse us of our past sins, so that we can be ruled out of Christian service; he likes to see the word 'failure' etched in our lives and hearts. But as we look in the way in which God dealt with Isaiah, we see a God who is not only holy but holy love. He forgives freely. His blood could cover up the sin of His prophet. Well can we sing with Charles Wesley, 'His blood can make the foulest clean; His blood avails for me.' We praise Him because we can be forgiven. And there's no meeting the sovereign and holy God until we meet Him at the cross where Jesus died for our sins.

Graham Kendrick wrote,

For us He was made sin,
Oh help me take it in!

Deep wounds of love cry out
'Father forgive'
...I worship, I worship the Lamb who was slain.

Thank God for that Lamb, for His grace, for His pardon, for His cleansing. Is there someone here who feels utterly rejected? You probably have the devil accusing you and saying you are a useless failure. How can you serve God? How dare you even come to Keswick? Don't believe his lies. God doesn't want you to grovel in unforgiven sins. He wants to free you, He wants to release you, He wants you to experience His joy and forgiveness. He doesn't want you to be wrapped up in the dark clouds of despair, He wants to shine His light on you so that you may be free to serve the living God.

But you and I must look with the inward gaze and allow God's light to shine into the dark recesses of our hearts. And when we confess our sin, and repent and claim the sacrificial blood of the Lord Jesus for cleansing and forgiveness, then we will be truly free. We will stand on our feet; we will be able to face God and we will be able to serve Him. And tonight God wants to say to you, 'Son, daughter, your sins have been forgiven.'

The outward gaze

In verse 8 God had some words to say to Isaiah. There is a council in the heavenly courts. Who will go for Us? Who will fulfil Our mission?

God couldn't have uttered those words before Isaiah was cleansed and forgiven. There's no point challenging obstinate, self-willed, arrogant sinners. But when hearts have been cleansed and freed from sin, when God has wrought His deep work of grace, then He has willing messengers.

Now God has tough assignments for the prophet. If you look at verse 9 onwards you find that he was to go to obstinate people, 'people who will hear and never understand, who see and never perceive'; whose hearts are hardened, whose senses are closed to God's word. Isn't that tough? Maybe it's how some of us are feeling tonight. God has tough assignments for us in His church, in the world. But He can only give the challenge to us, 'Who will go for us? Whom shall I send?' when our hearts are cleansed and renewed.

Isaiah's response was instant. 'Lord, here am I. Send me!' A few weeks ago John Gummer was talking about the Anglican Church as 'the church hesitant', and challenging the Archbishop of Canterbury, George Carey, to remember that the church is the church militant. But I want to suggest to you tonight that the churches that you and I represent are not only the church hesitant, we are the church reluctant. Have you ever tried to get people to serve, to evangelise, to visit, to minister? But when God touches us, when we have experienced His grace, we will become obedient. We are not to be the church reluctant, but the church obedient. Then we will be able to say to God, 'Lord here am I. Send me!'—not, 'Lord here am I. Send him! Send her!'

'I am ready, willing and able to serve You. I am available to bring Your gospel to the unchurched, to ethnic groups in our cities. I am available to pray, to be a prayer warrior, to care and visit the aged and lonely, to teach in a Sunday School, to encourage that struggling brother or sister, to do the leg-work in my church, to exercise my spiritual gifts.' Perhaps God is saying to some forgiven people tonight, 'Resign from the ranks of critics and complainers.' Having recently been in the pastorate I notice that there are many of them in our churches! Quit those ranks of critics and complainers, and get involved in Christian service. Be available, for there are great needs in the lost and needy world, and there are many things to fulfil and do in the church.

As we look out outward, we see a world of great need. But we need a strong incentive. What will send us out into this world? Again, we come back to the appreciation of what God has done for us in Jesus Christ.

Many years ago a medical missionary by the name of Dr Alexander Clark was working in the Congo—we call it Zaire today. There was no fresh food supply, so he and his fellow missionaries had to go hunting. One day in the jungle as he approached a clearing he saw a lion attacking and mauling an African. Dr Clark shot the lion, took the man back to the hospital and cared for him for many weeks until he recovered and went back to his tribe across the mountains.

Two or three months later Dr Clark was sitting on his veranda when he heard lots of noise. There was cackling of hens, noise of ducks, bleating of sheep and goats, and human noises; lots of children women and men. He went to see where the noise was coming from. In the distance was a tall African leading a procession chickens, ducks and geese, cows, goats and sheep, children, women, men. As he approached Dr Clark recognised him. The man ran towards the missionary doctor, fell at his feet and said, 'Sir, according to the law of our tribe, the man who has been rescued from the jaws of a wild beast no longer belongs to himself, he belongs to his rescuer. All that you see are yours, my chickens, ducks, geese are yours. My dogs, my sheep, my goats, my cows, they're yours. My servants are your servants, my children'—he had quite a few!—'are your children, and my wives'—he had several—'are your wives. Everything I have is yours. Because according to the law of our tribe, the man who has been rescued from the jaws of a wild beast no longer belongs to himself but to his rescuer.'

Brothers and sisters, you and I have been rescued from the jaws of hell, from the bondage of Satan by the Lord Jesus. We are not our own. We belong body, soul, mind, to the Lord Jesus Himself. Do we say to Him, 'Lord, all we are, all we have, all our resources, our time, our energy, are Yours. Use them where You will, when You will'? That should be our response when we look at Calvary and see how great God's love is for us in Jesus Christ. We sing with Isaac Watts,

> Were the whole realm of nature mine,
>   That were an offering far too small;
> Love so amazing, so divine,
>   Demands my soul, my life, my all.

'I saw the Lord.' Have you seen Him? Have you looked up? Have you had that upward gaze? Do you see God as sovereign and holy? Do you tremble and worship in His presence? Then, as you have seen God's holiness, His aweful purity, have you seen yourself, the sinfulness and wretchedness of your heart? God says to us 'Stop justifying your sin, stop giving excuses for your disobedience. Stop comparing yourselves with others.' Like David we have to say, 'It's against You that I have sinned and I am sorry. I repent.'

We have to recognise the wretchedness of our hearts, to cry to God for mercy, for forgiveness. Thank God! His pardon is always available to repentant sinners. Thank Him for His love and for His mercy as you look in.

Then as you look outwards to a world of great need, to a church that needs people to use their gifts for God's kingdom, God is saying to us, 'Look away from your own needs. Look outward at the lost and needy world, a world that desperately needs people to bring the good news of Jesus, a church that needs workers to use their resources time and talents for His kingdom.' He is saying to us, 'Do not withdraw. Do not sit on the sidelines of complacency. Get involved.'

May God's Spirit move us to say to Him, 'Lord, here am I. I am ready, willing and able. Lord here am I, send me.' And when we can pray that prayer and mean it, we will return to our churches and our homes, and we will be able to say to our friends truthfully, 'I saw the Lord, my eyes have seen the King, the Lord Almighty.'

'RESTORING THE YEARS'

by Rev. Tom Houston

Psalm 90:15

Monday is always the day in the Keswick Convention when we put the emphasis on sin. And I want to take an incident in the life of Hezekiah, a little-known man in the Old Testament who is nevertheless for me one of the key characters in the development of God's plan for His people.

Hezekiah was a king 2,700 years ago in Jerusalem. He was approaching forty years of age. He was married, his wife's name was Hephzibah, and so far there was no son and heir to the throne. Hezekiah had reigned for about fifteen years, coming to the throne in a dramatic way when he was twenty-five and leading his country in an astonishing programme of recovery in every aspect of national life. It's a real model for those who want to see the influence of the word of God on a nation. Trade flourished, finances improved, defences were strengthened, agriculture was developed, construction took place all over the country. Literature flourished and even the State religion thrived. In other words, it's almost the opposite of everything that we know in Britain today.

And Hezekiah, whose remarkable story you should read at your leisure, had been the pioneer in leading his country to that dramatic recovery. He had been very much his own man. He'd made it. He had come closer to his hero and model king David than any other ruler for three centuries. And then sickness struck.

It's not a well-known story. Who cares about Hezekiah or

Hephzibah anyway? The answer is that God cared; and somebody else cared enough to write it down. And if I understand the New Testament's perspective on the Old, these things happened to them for an example and were written down for our instruction. That's the key to the Old Testament.

And yet in a sense it's not so strange a story. It's a very familiar one, it happens all the time. It's probably happened or may even be happening to someone in this tent today; it will certainly happen to more of us as time goes on. This is not a unique incident. This is you and me at one point or other in our experience. Don't be like the foolish commentator who said that for 'more detailed information of the extent and nature of Hezekiah's reformation, we should have gladly have forgone the half-chapter on his boil.' That commentator missed the point entirely.

It was a matter of facing up to his mortality. We read about it not only in 2 Kings 20 but in Isaiah 38. Suddenly this forty-year old man is sick and it's terminal. His friend the prophet Isaiah visits him and confirms his own worst fears— 'The Lord says you are to put everything in order, because you will not recover. Get ready to die.'

What a bombshell! For him, but also for nation if they got to know of it. He had no heir. The national renewal was by no means complete; their enemies the Assyrians were threatening to invade—and here was the king on his death bed. And he was confronted with his own mortality. Let's see how he faced the crisis.

A few years ago I came home one evening from my work at the Bible Society. My wife had been reading a book that a friend had—presumably intentionally—left in our home. She said, 'You know, I think I understand you now as never before.' The book was called *Type A Behaviour and Your Heart*.[1] I read it and found I was a 'Type A': a classic candidate for a heart attack. What is a type A person? Well, Hezekiah was a type A person. The authors, two doctors, give four characteristics.

First is a sense of *time-urgency*. Type As are always trying to get more done in less time, setting deadlines and trying to meet them. Hezekiah's story is full of emphasis on time; as soon as he comes on to the page it is there. He begins work on the temple on New Year's Day (2 Chron. 29:3), works to a punishing schedule, and at the end (verse 36) there is rejoicing that it was done so quickly. He had that sense of time-urgency.

They are also *numbers* people. A Type A is always counting. How many stamps in my stamp collection, how many operations in a year, how much profit did I make? They sometimes even count the stairs as they go up and come down. Hezekiah was like that, too: he was a numbers man, he had his storerooms for gold and silver. A little later he got into trouble for bringing in the ambassadors from Babylon and showing them all that he had so carefully arranged (2 Kings 20, Isaiah 39). He had barns for his cattle and enclosures for his sheep, and even in 2 Kings 20 you hear 'three days', 'fifteen years', 'ten steps'. All the way with Hezekiah, it's numbers, numbers, numbers.

The third Type A characteristic is *insecurity about status*. Type A people are full of confidence, they don't give the impression of being insecure: but underneath, they are. In a crisis it comes out. Well, Hezekiah was in a crisis, and it came out: he describes it himself in the first part of the song of praise that he wrote after recovering from his illness (Isaiah 38). With all his astonishing achievements, you can sense in that song the underlying failure syndrome. Type A people have lost, or never had, any intrinsic yardstick by which to gauge their work to their own satisfaction. It's never enough, nothing is ever finished. That's what Hezekiah came up against when he was told he was going to die. 'My life,' he says, looking back on it, 'is cut off, ended, like a tent taken down.' What happens when a tent is taken down? All you have is some bruised grass, or in some countries trampled sands. And, 'My life was like a cloth cut from the loom'—a reject.

Those of you who are nurses; was this man a good patient? Listen to him: 'All night I cried out with pain as if a lion was breaking my bones. I thought God was ending my life, my voice was weak and I moaned like a dove. My eyes grew tired from looking to heaven. Lord, rescue me from all this trouble. What can I say? The Lord has done this, my heart is bitter, I can't sleep' (cf. Isa. 38). Would you like to nurse a man like that? The pain, the moaning, the tired eyes, the bitterness, the insomnia—where is great king Hezekiah now? All his confidence has evaporated in the face of sickness and possible death.

The fourth characteristic is *aggression and hostility*, a tendency always to compete with or to challenge other people. If you read the earlier part of the story and the parts following our passage this morning, you can see Hezekiah facing his challengers and see where his competitiveness got him.

This Type A man is up against it and not doing well.

Isn't it a familiar story? When sickness strikes, the body doesn't respond as it used to, the mind is overcome with depression. You can't move and you have thoughts you can't control. All you worked to acquire cannot help you now. Your values somehow get stood on their head, and the reckoning leaves us very short. Sir Walter Scott asked, 'Is death the last sleep? No, it is the final awakening.' Hezekiah was awakening to reality as he faced death. The psychologist Freud said, 'No one believes in his own death. In the unconscious, everyone is convinced of his immortality.' We live as if we are going to live for ever.

Our society conspires to keep up the fiction by not talking openly about death and by relegating it to the hospital and the mortuary. But death is real and death is certain. It's been said that the denial of death is one cause of empty and purposeless lives, that when one recognises that each day might be one's last, one takes time to grow and reach out to others. Death is the only certain fact of life, as Hezekiah discovered at age forty. It was terrible. But he was not completely overcome. After his friend Isaiah had confirmed the verdict he turned his face to the wall—a gesture of acceptance—and made a good attempt at a prayer of resignation. But he couldn't put a brave face on it. He began to cry bitterly as he faced up to his mortality. But he did it.

So must we. And God will see that we do it, sooner or later. The Bible is open and realistic about death. It encourages us to face the fact of it. It also tells us the significance of death, the final awakening, the bottom line, the calling to account, the evaluation. We need to face up to our mortality. And when we do, one of our greatest fears leaves us. I maintain death is one of the two fears—death and poverty—of which you must be rid to be really equipped for life. And Hezekiah was facing the first.

Why wait for sickness to make us face up to our mortality? Is that not what Keswick conventions are for, to take stock of our lives? If we lived no longer, what would our lives so far add up to? Have the locusts been busy in our lives?

The miracle of the restored years

After praying a rather pathetic prayer, he wept. It was not a very great prayer. But God heard it and he sent Isaiah back to say so. 'And God saw his tears.' Isn't that a great truth? God hears our prayers and sees our tears. 'Is any man among you afflicted? Let him pray,' said James. And Hezekiah did, and God sent back the very man who had confirmed his worst fears to announce a reprieve. 'In three days you'll be back in the temple. You'll have fifteen years added to your life.'

It seems a significant period. Fifteen years was roughly the same period he had reigned. It was almost like a chance to do it all again, but better. How often we would like to have that chance! In Psalm 90:15 the psalmist prays, 'Make us glad as many days as you have afflicted us, for as many years as we have seen trouble.'

This is what Joel is getting at when he records 'I will restore to you the years that the locusts have eaten—the great locust and the young locust, the other locusts and the locust swarm—my great army that I sent to you' (2:25). I haven't been close to locusts, but they did once come and eat everything green in our garden when we lived in Africa. It was just the fringe of a plague of locusts, but you never saw green stuff disappear as fast as when these little things got going. And when army worms—little brown small caterpillars that come like an army through a region and eat everything green in their path—came into our garden, we had a nice lawn one day and just soil the next day. And I imagine that's how someone here might see the years they've lived; years that the locusts have eaten. Not a lot to show for them.

The locusts of self-indulgence, of the search for pleasure, of sin and dishonesty, of voyeurism and creeping lust, secret sin and deceitfulness; the army worms of apathy and laziness are just waiting and delaying and procrastinating—waiting for someone or something all the time, putting off the thing that needs to be done. The question is not 'How green is my valley?' but 'How brown is my valley?'. We need to face up to our mortality.

About a year ago I was meeting with the elders of a church in Nairobi. We got on to a perennial topic: why are men not so prominent in the church as women, and why is it more difficult to get them to do things in the church apart from attending? There was a brother there from Ghana. He said, 'I don't know about Kenya but I can tell you what we think in Ghana. When people enter business and public life in Ghana they have to do things that they know violate the Christian ethic. They feel they would be letting the side down if they were prominent in the church when they were behaving like that in business. You know what they do? They wait till they retire before they get active in the church.'

Isn't that a good illustration of the years that the locusts are eating? That's our question for tonight: Will our lives move on in the deteriorating direction they have been going—or will there be a pause and a reversal? Will the future be as the past has been, or will the future be as the Lord can make it if we put our lives in His hands? We can choose. God engages us in the decision; He wants us to choose.

Peter denied his Lord three times. But Jesus came back after the resurrection and gave him three opportunities—a very delicate gentle way of saying 'I want to blot out the past, the future can be different.' He commissioned him again. And the Lord was doing that with Hezekiah.

And we too can choose. God engages us in the decision; He wants us to contemplate the sundial of our life, and give Him freedom to do some reversing of trends that will make it like a return from the shadows of evening to the brightness of the noon day. God did this for Hezekiah, but He did it for the people's sake (2 Kings 20:6). Our prayers are answered because God cares for those who are affected by our lives and for His own name's sake, not because we are special in some exceptional way. And so he was told: You can have fifteen years more. What a reprieve that was! The miracle of life restored.

Yet there's a sad note to all of this. George Adam Smith describes this story as 'An Old Testament believer's death bed, and the difference Jesus makes'. For as we read the rest of his psalm we find that Hezekiah had at that time no hope of an afterlife. That changed with Jesus and the resurrection. He brought life and immortality; and we need not only to accept the significance of His death, but we to accept the fact and gift of eternal life through Jesus Christ our Lord. That is the gospel, and we may have the miracle of life restored in a life of new eternal quality, when we accept it as a gift from God.

But for Hezekiah it all hinged on a question. 2 Kings 29, 'Would you prefer the shadow on the stairway to go forward ten steps or back ten steps?' (2 Kings 29). He was offered a sign and he had to choose. I imagine he could see the sundial in the garden from the window of the room where he lay. It would be a little pyramid of steps, with a short pillar or obelisk on top, built by his father Ahaz. And in the morning the shadow would fall down on the west side to the very bottom of the steps, to the lowest step. And gradually it would shrink up the steps with the rising of the sun, until at noon it was at the foot of the little obelisk in the centre; and afterwards the shadow crept down the east side. Each step was one degree of time. The story takes place during the afternoon, when the shadow was lengthening towards him. To Hezekiah, dying, the lengthening shadow was like the finger of death coming nearer.

'Do you want a sign that you will be well? Do you want the shadow to go forward ten steps or back ten steps?' And Hezekiah said—I hope you hear it—'It is easy for the shadow to go forward ten steps.'

Ivor Lewis was a Welsh preacher who came to Glasgow while I was a teenager and a budding preacher. He announced this subject for one of his meetings: 'What must I do to be lost?' As a young preacher I thought that was a great sermon title. I went along to hear him. He began his sermon by proclaiming in his Welsh accent, 'What must I do to be lost? Nothing!' His text was 'How shall we escape if we neglect so great salvation'. What does neglect mean? It means, to do nothing. It is easy for the shadow to go for- wards. It will be easy for you to go out tonight and your life to continue as it has been. It is easy for the shadow to go forward.

But Hezekiah prayed for it to go backward, and it did. And he had the same number of years added as he had already reigned.

There's another critical example of this experience in the Bible that I want to refer to briefly. It's in the life of Moses. Did you know, Moses wrote a psalm? It's Psalm 90. I calcu- late that he must have written it towards the end of his time herding cattle in the desert and just before his experience at the burning bush. If that's so, for nearly forty years his talents had been wasted. His early dreams had been shattered, his rich experience in the court of Pharoah was unproductive, and life was a long drawn-out disappointment for this servant of God—all because of impulsive impatience, when he thought he was in his prime. He struggled with it all, as we see in Psalm 90. And he came to a critical point—was it all finished, had he blown it completely, was he deservedly on the shelf?—it was very easy to come to self-pity and think it was all over. But no, in the psalm he tells us even though he had experienced the anger of God, he sees again the steadfast love of God. And he prays, 'Make us glad for as many days as you have afflicted us' (Psalm 90:15). And God did. He gave him forty years of leadership after the forty years of obscurity in the desert. And how important that was in the whole history of salvation; what a preparation for the burning bush! Even then he was rather reluctant, you may remember. But that leadership of Moses hinged on his reaction to the wasted years in the desert. There was an inward spark left. He wanted more. He wanted the shadow to go back, not to go forward.

What about you? What about me? You know, there's another shadow that Hezekiah did not know anything about in his day. It's the shadow of the cross. That shadow larger than the sundial of all our wasted years. It towers over the sins of greed, conceit, impulse, failure, manipulation, envy, derision and above all unbelief. The shadow of the cross is not a shadow to run from. It is a shadow to run into, for therein all our sins are swallowed up and covered, never to appear again.

How often have you sung, 'Beneath the cross of Jesus, I fain would take my stand...A rest upon the way, from the burning of the noontide heat and the burden of the day'? The heaviness, the weariness of the day. There's a weariness in Christian circles today. Do you feel it? Is it in you? Is it getting to you? Maybe you know what it is to have a wilderness experience.

There lies beneath its shadow
    But on the farther side,
The darkness of an awful grave
    That gapes both deep and wide:
And there between us stands the cross,
    Two arms outstretched to save,
Like a watchman set to guard the way
    From that eternal grave.

I take, O cross, thy shadow,
    For my abiding place;
I ask no other sunshine than
    The sunshine of His face:
Content to let the world go by,
    To know no gain nor loss,
My sinful self, my only shame,
    My glory all the cross.

Do you prefer the shadow to go forward or to go back?

Hezekiah said, go back; and he was given as many years as he had had before.

The song of a restored person

He ends with the song of a restored person: 'Lord, I will live for you for ever' (cf. Isaiah 38:16-20). He had a new centre in his life, a new contentment. That's what happens when the shadow goes back: bitterness goes out and peace comes in.

What a terrible thing it is to live with bitterness and resentment and an unforgiving spirit.

And sometimes that's the question: Will the shadow go back? Are we ready to forgive? Recently a television programme contrasted two women who had both been badly abused. They were talking about forgiveness. One was a vicar's daughter who had been raped while her father and her fiancé were being beaten up: and she was ready to forgive the person. And there was a woman who had been mugged, and had no forgiveness in her heart. She just wanted the person to get everything that was coming to him.

It was quite a sensitive programme. But I wish the presenter had kept two things separate. The question was raised as to whether 'justice needed to be done'. Of course justice needs to be done. The presenter hadn't realised that it is not a case of Christians forgiving, and everybody else seeking justice. The Christian doesn't forgive because the other person repents. There's only one reason: that is, because he or she is already forgiven. 'I forgive you, because Christ has forgiven me.' That's the sequence. That's why forgiveness has to be unconditional, and that's what gets the bitterness out.

But Jesus went so far as to say that if the forgiven person is not a forgiver, then they are not a forgiven person after all. It blocks the flow.

Hezekiah had a new contentment: peace instead of bitterness, a new confidence. God was his protector. He had a new continuity. He had the sense of the flow of generations. 'Fathers tell their children about your faithfulness' (verse 19). He was back in the line of succession of believing people. And it was a continual celebration of what God has done— 'Lord you have healed me, we will play harps and sing your praise and sing praise in your temple as long as we live.'

The most important thing that you need to know about the rest of your life is that today is the first day of the rest of your life. And I believe that today is a pivotal day for some here.

Isaiah prayed to the Lord and the Lord made the shadow go back. 'Take words with you and return to the Lord,' said Hosea (Hos. 14:2). Are you ready to pray or have someone to pray for you? I cannot tell you what to pray. Only you know the words. But take words with you and return to the Lord. Maybe it can only be tears, maybe it's already gone beyond words, and there's a fountain of the great deep waiting to burst within you that would bring you back, to begin to see those years that the locusts have eaten, those years that have been afflicted by weariness and staleness and barrenness, change to fruitfulness.

Do you know what one of the greatest criticisms is that can be made of us Christians? People say we're boring. Sometimes I think they're right, because there's a weariness amongst us, a staleness. It's not meant to be like that.

'I will restore the years the locusts have eaten.'

'Take words with you and return to the Lord.'

Note

1. Meyer Friedman and Ray H. Rosenman, *Type A Behaviour and Your Heart* (USA: Fawcett, 1985).

'A POSTSCRIPT FOR PREACHERS'

by Dr Raymond Brown
(Ministers' Meeting, Convention Week)

John 21

I am now in my last year of full-time pastoral ministry. Consequently I have found myself inevitably in a slightly reflective mood, thinking back about ministry and priorities and values—like all of us, I suppose, embarrassed about things I could have done better and somewhat haunted by great things I might or should have done. But as I've reflected I've found myself returning to a passage to which I felt drawn since I first knew I was to speak at this meeting. It's a very familiar passage; you've all preached on it; and I don't presume for a moment to say anything new about it. But I want to think with you about the last chapter of John's Gospel. I think there is something very special about this passage, coming as it does as a kind of epilogue; and I'd love to share a few things with you about ministry, and what it may be saying to us in today's world.

What a marvellous passage it is! And how extraordinary to add this epilogue, when John already had the most brilliant ending possible for his Gospel—what more compelling, attractive and spiritually challenging better ending to any Gospel could there be than a group of disciples, met together in the upper room, hearing the words of Jesus, 'Peace be to you'? What better ending than the reminder that He died for them, as He shows them His hands and side, as He encourages them to understand that they are to go out and share that good news of His saving death and resurrection with other people—'As the Father has sent me even so send I you'? What better ending than the encouragement that though the task will be demanding, they won't have to do it in their own strength and their own energy, for—anticipating Pentecost—Jesus breathes on them and says, 'Receive the Holy Spirit' (John 20:22)?

Just as in Ezekiel's vision breath brought life, these bewildered disciples are assured that there will be the necessary dynamism for this ministry in the world. They are given authority to give people the assurance that if their sins are forgiven in Christ, then truly they are forgiven. And one, a doubter who is not present at the meeting—a feature that they will meet scores if not hundreds and hundreds of times later in their ministry—is brought to faith. The Gospel reaches a majestic ending as this man who had not been present and heard those great things, but now comes to believe that Jesus is truly alive, falls on his knees, makes the great Christian confession, 'My Lord and my God', and acknowledges at the close of the Gospel the deity of Christ with which this marvellous book began. What an ending!

I am convinced that initially John intended to finish at verses 30-31. I would like to ask him: 'Did you intend to finish with that majestic call to faith at the end, "Believe that Jesus is the Christ, the Son of God?" ' For suddenly it all starts again. 'Afterwards Jesus appeared again' (21:1). It's a mercy, isn't it, that even after the most wonderful mountain-top experiences when we have been intimately aware of the nearness, power, sufficiency and supremacy of Jesus—Jesus comes again. They are not once-and-for-all affairs, locked up in our spiritual biography somewhere. Jesus keeps making Himself known to us.

And I am convinced that this story is really about ministers, about servants. It's a kind of addendum to the Gospel, of course intended for every reader, but it says something very special to workers, disciples—fishermen if you like—shepherds who will have a renewed commission; and to followers, martyrs, witnesses, who may have to pay the price of blood for their faithfulness to Jesus. And I think the narrative has something quite special to say to us as ministers and leaders and workers (and partners of such people in the

Lord's work) about some of the tensions and pressures which these earlier followers and servants of Christ had, and how they coped with them. I want therefore to begin with some of the issues that may have been at stake; some of the difficulties that were experienced by these early servants of Christ: the minister's tensions. And then we will consider the minister's Lord, for all the tensions were met in Jesus.

The minister's tensions

Coping with flatness

Peter's sudden decision to go fishing has puzzled expositors. It may just have been the need to earn some money for food. But I think it could be that after those wonderful meetings with Christ, when Jesus came to them through closed doors, now that they were waiting for Him in Galilee as He'd told them to, Peter wanted to fill the gap. He, of all people, is an activist. He has to be doing something, he has to say something to meet the situation. He wants to fill up the time now because he's coping with bewilderment. 'Jesus said He was going to meet us—"I'm going ahead of you into Galilee"— Why isn't He here? Why hasn't Christ come into this situation?'

Perhaps it was that which gave Peter the impulse to say, 'I'm going fishing.' He knew the ropes, he could soon get back into it. He'd laid it aside for the past three years, but there were other fishermen there, the sons of Zebedee, who would join him in the boat. As far as we know, the others were not fishermen. John tells us that Nathanael came from miles inland; the story of how he met Christ suggests that he was something of a student, perhaps even with a rabbinical training—'When you were under the fig tree' was a rabbinical expression of a student of the law. I've no reason to imagine Thomas was a fisherman either, and we don't know about the other two disciples. But they were swept along with the idea and went into the boat that night because—well, they were filling up the time too, rather perplexed about what was going to happen next. How marvellous if the Christ who said, 'I am going ahead of you into Galilee,' would actually meet them that night! But He hadn't turned up.

There are times in the Lord's work when we have to cope

with a sense of flatness, emptiness, ordinariness; when we wish that Jesus would appear again freshly in our situation. We've worked hard at it, but Oh! we'd love a break. Something that would indicate to us that the Lord is certainly with us, really blessing us, that people's lives are being touched. But we've just got to do the same things over again, faithfully expounding the word. Yet don't you wish for a response sometimes? Don't you long that you will see the fruit that other ministers talk a lot about? You've examined your own heart, you're not remotely jealous—but why isn't it happening to you?

I remember hearing a minister talking about his time in his church. I went to preach for him at the service that marked the end of his full-time ministry, and he said how he came to that church and felt for a long time as if it were a great big aircraft lumbering along the runway. Then he said, 'But don't you remember that exciting moment when you take off? The plane's racing along the runway, and all of a sudden you realise it's off the ground. There's a real lift.'

I thought to myself: Yes, I would love that too, that 'real sense of lift'. You don't always have it. Sometimes you just have to slog it out, just waiting for Jesus to break in in a very special way. You know that He's there, that He will bless, that the word will be honoured, that there will be fruit. But you don't always see it happening.

Coping with bewilderment

We preach so much, understandably, about the biblical material where God is always doing something special in somebody's life. It's easy to think it was always like that for all of them. But Jacob didn't always see a ladder set between earth and heaven. Every bush in the desert wasn't aflame with fire for Moses; there must have been some ghastly days when he just had to plod on with all that grumbling crowd behind him. It must have been awful. There were times for Elijah when he didn't hear the still small voice, 'the sound of a gentle stillness'. There were moments when he was down and discouraged. It wasn't every day that Jeremiah saw the almond rod blossoming, the waker after the death of winter as they called it—the first sign of Spring: 'I will waken my word to perform it.' In fact Jeremiah's story, from a human perspective, isn't a success story at all. It's only a success story from an eternal perspective. Here am I, in an English Lakeland town, talking about it centuries after his death; yet there must have been many times when he wondered whether it was all worthwhile. He said so: 'You've dealt with me as a deceitful brook, as waters that fail.'

The heavens weren't always open towards the exiled Ezekiel. For all these great people in Old Testament and New Testament times, there must have been days when they just had to slog it out, press on and work at their best for the Lord, and trust Him and pray and believe and hope. Paul wasn't always lifted up to the third heaven. Sometimes he was in prison. But he went on and on. We've got to remember, that the Lord Jesus will come to us and He will appear even when coping with bewilderment is tough. Why hasn't Jesus come, why isn't He manifesting Himself now? That question drove Peter out to fish.

Coping with disappointment

I sometimes wonder what they thought about that night, as time and again they slid their fingers into the nets hoping to find a heavy haul but finding virtually nothing there. Don't you think it was deliberate, the act of the majestic Lord of nature as well as of history, performing the great miracle of keeping the fish out of the net just because He wanted a re-run of day and a night three years earlier when they'd toiled all night on that lake and told Him, 'We caught nothing, nothing at all'?

I wonder whether those seven men in that boat looked at each other and reflected on the past. Here they were coping not just with bewilderment but with disappointment; disappointment with themselves. It was a strange collection when you think about it. Peter the coward, Thomas the doubter, Nathanael the one-time cynic ('Can any good thing come out of Nazareth?'), the two sons of Zebedee—well, they had their moments when they were certainly not at their best: the ambitious men who wanted special thrones in the eternal glory; the loveless men who, if Samaritan homes would not give them hospitality considered that perhaps they should be burnt. And two other disciples—we don't know what their failings would be. Perhaps they are deliberately anonymous so that we can think not about ours instead. Maybe they could look at each other say, 'Well, I'm not the only one who's made a mess of things in the past; I think some of these have as well.'

Sometimes that's one of the difficult things about the ministry. Not just coping with disappointment about yourself, but coping realistically, sensitively, with disappointment about other people. You've been let down, and you of all people are aware of their failings; not that you want to expose them, but sometimes you look not just at yourself but at the team around you and you're disappointed. It's happened with many servants of Christ.

Here they were. They weren't a team, they weren't anything like they could or should have been, they'd all failed in the past and made ghastly mistakes. But Jesus was going to appear to them. He was going to make Himself known to people who were coping with disappointment.

Coping with failure

They couldn't even do the one thing that some of them thought they could do best—fishing. Half of them were experienced fishermen, they'd hauled in nets scores of times and on that lake too. They knew the best places to catch fish and sell it. But even the thing that they thought they could do well, they couldn't do at all.

Was it so that Jesus could impress them through their failure, and remind them of some marvellous words that Jesus said and John, who was in the boat, recorded: 'Without me you can do nothing'? Oh yes, it was natural for them to go out and fill up the time, but Jesus wanted them to know that their success in the future would be totally and utterly dependant upon Him.

Coping with guilt

The sensitive minister or Christian worker knows all about coping with guilt. You're far more concerned over the things you haven't done well or things you've done badly. Do you want to spend most of your time finding faults with other people? But like Peter you're aware of your own failings. And isn't this another quite deliberate re-run that we've all talked about and preached about? It may be, in the mercy of

Christ, not only reminding them of the great success story at the beginning of the ministry—the magnificent catch in Luke 5, the best they'd ever seen yet they gave it up for Jesus—nor only reminding them of the moments of success, and high resolve, and devotion. Wasn't it saying something to Peter about failure, about not being surrounded by success and partners who were as excited as he was about all that Christ had done? Alone in that garden, or surrounded by enemies; feeling smaller and smaller because he'd let Jesus down, feeling worse and worse as the minutes ticked by; coping with guilt.

And doesn't Jesus, in His magnificent love, want to bring him to the point where he can openly confess to it, so that he knows he is completely forgiven? Isn't that why the fire was burning on the shore, so that standing by the fire he'd be reminded of what had happened those few nights before? Wasn't the threefold commission to Peter intended to recall that? The conversation was all about love. 'Do you love Me really, more than the other six here? You said you did. You said everybody could leave you; the other five might run away but you wouldn't. You were ready to go with Me to prison and to death. Do you really love Me more than these others? Do you really love Me?'

'Jesus—you know that I love you.'

The Lord Jesus is surely even pressing it home by the very way that He addresses him: 'Simon, son of John'. Not Peter, but the name that was given to him at the beginning of this Gospel and by which he was known at their very first meeting—just to take him back to the beginning and to help him to see how desperately he needed the Saviour in the future. And the very words that Jesus said to him: 'I tell you the truth, Amen, amen'—the double amen, 'I say to you'—are recorded in this Gospel when Jesus talked to him in chapter 6 about his certain denial. 'I tell you the truth Peter, you will deny me.' It was all surely an intended deliberate re-run, so that this man could face his guilt. 'Jesus, you know that I love you. You know that I'm better at heart than my worst words, however dreadful they may have been in the garden.'

I believe that one reason this story is told is to show that even this man, who was to be prince among preachers and was to draw thousands at Pentecost, could fail. But he could be restored.

Coping with possessiveness

Is there not something quite deliberate about Jesus' command? 'Feed My lambs...feed My sheep...take care of My sheep...feed My sheep. They're not yours, they're Mine.'

That's why Peter, when towards the end of his days he writes to all the churches scattered around Asia Minor, comes back to this: 'Tend the flock of God—it's not yours—which is in your charge. Yes, you're responsible but you don't own it.' We need to be reminded of that, don't we? Innocently, sometimes even affectionately we can talk about 'my people'. That's all right—as long as we don't ever feel we do own them. They all belong to Him, and that means He has full control over every part of them. We mustn't talk about them, deal with them or speak to them as if in any sense they're our property to push around. They are His sheep.

Coping with costliness

Peter was in a very unusual position. He knew as no other person knows that he would become an old man. Life was going to stretch out ahead of him, and there were going to be many years, perhaps thirty, in which he could serve Jesus. But he would certainly walk the way of the cross. 'You're young, Peter. You know what it is to get up and get dressed and order your own life, but a day will come when they will take you and carry you where you do not want to go.' He said this to indicate the kind of death by which Peter would glorify God. Peter knew from that moment that, in the end, blood would be shed.

Coping with preoccupation

But even after hearing that call of Christ to follow Him, even in the way of the cross, Peter is just a little intrigued about the spiritual welfare of someone else. Isn't there a lovely naturalness about the story, a gorgeous humanity? That is why I love Scripture and am so convinced of its reliability and authority. If we'd have been asked to record some of these events described in God's word there are many people and events we'd have left out. You want to say the best of people;

you don't want this in. 'What shall this man do?'—it wasn't any of Peter's business. But how natural!

Perhaps at times, only occasionally, we lose that essential balance between our own spirituality—the need to go into the quiet place and spend time with God, to make sure that we're right and can really look Him in the eye and say to Him, 'Lord, you know that I love you'—and the natural responsibility we have for others. He did say, 'Feed my sheep—care for others.' And here was Peter just a little bit concerned about John and what was going to happen to him. 'What shall this man do?' It's not easy to get that balance. Of course we've got to look after other people's spiritual welfare. Of course there must be ministry, good exposition of Scripture, visiting of the people of God, commitment to the work, constant thought for the needs of others. And if you're a sensitive person, coming to the end of a week and haunted by the things you might and ought and could have done, it all dwarfs an enormous amount that actually you have done. And in those moments you can feel low. We've got to keep the balance between our own walk with Him and our own work for Him. There's a terrible danger of preoccupation with other people's spiritual life to the neglect of our own.

When I first came as a young airman to the Keswick Convention I was an active, very young Christian. I'd only been converted about two years. But I ran a youth club, I was a Sunday School teacher, I was going out preaching, and trying my best to witness for Christ in the opportunities that came to me. I was involved in tract distribution. I used to lead the singing at the evangelistic meeting every week. I can't believe it now! My diary was crammed.

In that huge tent on the Monday evening I heard W. H. Aldiss give an address that's pursued me all my days. He spoke from the opening chapter of the Song of Solomon: 'They made me keeper of the vineyards, but my own vineyard have I not kept.' It spoke to me. I was so busy in the Lord's work that the only thing I wasn't looking after was my own inner life with Christ. There was so much activity, and it was good activity; but I was neglecting my own devotional life.

'What shall this man do?' Well, what shall I do? Tell Jesus I love Him, and spend time with Him, surely.

The minister's Lord

So much for the disciples. What did they learn about the Lord?

I think the key to the chapter is in verse 7, in the words of the disciple whom Jesus loved—literally 'The Lord it is!' It's another announcement of the lordship of Christ. It had been there in the words of Mary—'I have seen the Lord!' (20:18). It was the words of Thomas—'My Lord and my God!' (20:28). It was the words of the disciples, whom Thomas could not believe—'We have seen the Lord!' (cf. 20:25). And of the disciple whom Jesus loved who says, 'The Lord it is!'

He's spoken to them so lovingly, that stranger on the shore. It's a very warm friendly word that He used—translated 'friends', it's a homely kind of word that would have meant so much to a group of Galilean men in that boat. 'Lads, have you got anything, have you caught anything?' The disciple whom Jesus loved knew it was the Lord Jesus. And in this run of events I believe there are a whole sequence of factors that were saying things about His lordship that would help them in the days that were to come—dark, difficult, painful and costly days for some of them.

Holy in His person

What about when Peter first heard that word? 'The Lord it is!' Impetuous Peter again—'I'm going fishing', 'What shall this man do?'—but at that moment he showed he really did love Jesus. He leapt into the water, but not until he'd thrown his robe about him. I think there's something special about that. Wasn't that a strange action for somebody who was about to plunge into the water—to weigh yourself down with extra clothing? Well, yes. But if you were going into the presence of the most wonderful person in the world, wouldn't you want to be properly robed? When they said, 'The Lord it is!' Peter, for all his impulsiveness, wanted to go into the presence of Jesus and be at his best, recognising that the Lord is holy in His person.

Generous in His provision
They arrived and there was their breakfast. The Lord already
had a meal partly prepared for them, the fire, the bread, the
fish. He'd gone ahead of them. We have always to remember
that. The Lord Jesus is always ahead of us, however tough
and difficult it is; there always will be the generous provision
we need.

'Bring some of the fish you've caught.' And they sat down
so excited about the fish, the miracle that the nets hadn't
broken, the re-run again of Luke 5. But this time they
counted them—153 fish. The expositors over the years have
had a good time with the 153 fish. They did in the patristic
period. Jerome believed that it was 153 because the Greek
zoologists said that there were 153 different varieties of fish to
be found in the sea. Augustine said the answer was not in
zoology but mathematics; 153 is the sum of 1+2+3+4 right
through to 17. It's true, Augustine was right. But surely what
it signifies is that there were a lot of fish. They were there in
abundance. We are told they were large fish, so many that it
was a miracle the net didn't break. But then, this is the
Gospel in which Jesus does everything in superlative abundance—'Of his fullness have all we received and grace for
grace' (1:16, AV). We're not short of anything in this Gospel,
that's surely what it means. It was a huge catch, a marvellous
meal, far more than they could ever eat. Jesus always gives
you everything you need and more than anything you need.
The well is within you, you don't have to go and draw your
water as the woman did at Jacob's well. It's within you, a well
of water springing up into eternal life, you'll never ever thirst
again.

There may be just an echo here of the bread and the fish of
John 6—'He took the bread and gave it to them and did the
same with the fish.' Perhaps even in that moment they were
being reminded that there was enough then for everyone and
so much that there was a huge amount left for people who
were not present, who could be fed from the baskets that
were taken away. It's this Gospel that says not only that you
should have joy, but that you should have it to the full. 'Not
as the world gives do I give to you' (cf. 14:27).

How does the world give? The world of His day gave it as

a greeting, 'Shalom'. It was a word, it fell easily from the lips. The Romans used a word, too: *pax*. Actually the *pax Romana* was far from peaceful but cruel, vindictive and aggressive—crucified people, people put out of their homes, their goods plundered. Peace was just a word. Augustus, the first Roman emperor, erected a great altar to peace in Rome. Peace indeed! There was cruelty. In some parts of the world, of course, stability and security: but Jesus says, 'I'm not giving to you a name, an idea. I'm giving you peace, and it's peace when everything else around you is in turmoil and you're in real hardship and suffering.' This is the Gospel where the jars of water are filled to the brim. It's fullness. 'I have come that you might have life and you might have it to the full.'

This story tells us that the Lord is holy in His person. Never forget it. We want to come before Him and ask Him that we might be at our best. Only He can make us at our best: clothed not in our poor rags, but in the robes of His own righteousness. Longing to be at our best for Him, and thanking Him for the generosity of His provision and His loving care, meeting these needs.

Searching in His judgement

He is searching in His judgement. Oh yes, seeing us as we really are, looking into Peter's face by the firelight of the early morning; but looking in a very different way from how the girl had looked at Him. Remember that graphic detail in the Passion narrative—she's looking at him very intently in the firelight. 'I think you're a Galilean, you were with Him, we've seen you with Him.' Jesus looked at him in the firelight of the early morning, but not like that. He looked at him and through him, knew everything about him, but loved him. He didn't just ask for Peter's love but offered him the love that would last for ever: the Son of God who loved him and gave Himself for him.

Unlimited in His knowledge

'There's no need to put these questions to me, Lord. You know everything.' Yes He did, He knew everything about Peter, all his mistakes in the past. He knew everything about this other disciple and what would happen to him in the future. He knew that Peter would walk the way of martyrdom.

What an assuring, deeply comforting thing that is, that Jesus knows all about us. He knows the past and all our failures. He knows the present and our potential, knows the future and its challenge. He loves us deeply just the same.

Supreme in His sovereignty
He is precise in His priorities, calling him to service, to care for the flock of God in the future. But He is supreme in His sovereignty. He knows what He's doing with His men and His women. One of them He is sending clearly and unmistakably the way of the cross, the way of martrydom. And I wouldn't dogmatise that John is the disciple whom Jesus loved, but perhaps for him it was almost a tougher ordeal—Patmos, isolation, separation, being away from the people of God.

But the disciples knew. 'The Lord it is!'

And if that's so, they're safe in His strong hands. What a blessing it is to belong to Jesus. What a wonderful privilege to serve Him. And what a great thing it is to know that whatever our difficulties, He is the one who can help us to cope with them! He does it by reassuring us and telling us 'The Lord it is!'

He is present always, sometimes when we least expect it. He must have been on the shore long before they saw Him. We must never forget it.

'A LIVING HOPE'

by Canon Keith Weston

1 Peter 1:3

What I want to talk about with you is the fruit that results from Jesus' life, death and resurrection. In John 12:24 Jesus says, 'Truly, truly, I say to you, unless a grain of wheat falls into the earth and dies, it remains alone; but if it dies it bears much fruit.' The context? Verse 23: 'The hour has come for the Son of man to be glorified.' Surely therefore the reference in verse 24 is to that grain of wheat our Lord and Saviour, falling into the ground and dying. But in dying He bears much fruit; so He bears fruit in redeemed lives, and He looks for the fruit of our redemption. But I want to take you back a stage, to that cross and to that tomb on that first Easter Day. Because that's where the grain—with a lovely capital G—the Grain of wheat died and bore fruit.

In 1 Peter 1 we have a very precious passage of the New Testament. As you read it, listen for one word which, I believe, sums up this fruit of the Passion of the Lord Jesus, His cross and His resurrection. It is the word 'hope', and it occurs three times in verses 3, 13 and 21. The seeds, so to speak, of His death and resurrection bring forth this fruit of a real and living hope for all who will trust in Christ; a hope which because of His dying for us looks back over the past, and breaks into the misery of our sinful failure with new and glorious hope of forgiveness of sins, of being 'ransomed' (verse 18)—not with silver and gold but with the precious blood of Christ.

And it is a hope that not only looks back and redeems us from our sinful past but gloriously looks into the future and opens up a vista of glory for us, the fruit of His dying and rising again. As Peter says in verse 3, a 'living hope'. How? Through the resurrection of Jesus Christ from the dead. And so our salvation looks back and says that all that past is blotted out and forgiven, through faith in Christ and His finished work upon the cross. Hallelujah! And the future opens up with a wonderful living hope through the resurrection of Jesus Christ from the dead, a hope which takes you over death into glory. Hallelujah!

I've really given you my talk, because that's a summary of all I want to say! But let me fill it out for you.

Margaret and I have retired since last year's Keswick— that's why we look so liberated. My sell-by date passed last July—I hope I've still got some shelf life left. Last summer we collected the key to our retirement semi—the first home we've ever owned. And we went through that awful trauma of buying a house and moving, getting rid of all those books and furniture. Trying to squeeze possessions into a very small semi really is one of the great traumas of life. But what a happy thought: it's our last move! The next move will be to heaven, and not to a semi-detached house on a housing estate, but, says John 14, to a mansion. Someone else will have to bother about the books and belongings we leave behind. Do you know that lovely line in the hymn, 'For ever with the Lord, Amen, so let it be...We nightly pitch our moving tent a day's march nearer home'?

That's part of the glorious fruit of the death and resurrection of Jesus, a living hope through the resurrection of Jesus, and a wonderful hope because all the past has been dealt with and future is glorious indeed. A hope that embraces all that there is of life. Isn't that wonderful?

But how many there are in our society who simply do not think that way. Just last week an old school friend, who was a senior when I was a junior, came to have coffee with us. In his old age he has learned to write poetry. He gave us a volume of his poems, which are lovely. Let me give you an example of one of them. It's called 'The Sceptic'.

The caterpillar asked his friend,
'When we pupate, is that the end?
I met some people who contend
    We have a life to come;
They seem quite sure that you and I
Will grow two pairs of wings and fly,
And dance all day around the sky—
    It all sounds rather rum!'

His friend replied: 'Two pairs of wings?
I wonder where they hear such things!
They tell you their imaginings
    Like those who really know.
To fly! That would be quite a trick!
Our bodies are too coarse and thick;
For that, you must be very quick,
    And we are far too slow.

'It may be pleasant to recall,
And tell the grubs while they are small,
It's a story far too tall
    For likes of you and me.
Beware the webs that people weave,
Whose far-fetched fantasies deceive;
A caterpillar should believe
    What he can taste and see.

'So trouble not your little head
With what will happen when you're dead,
But spend your energies instead
    On things that we can chew;
Our place it is to crawl and feed,
To satisfy our natural greed,
To fatten, and pay no heed
    To what may not be true.'[1]

It's very sad, though rather nicely put. Isn't it the way so many people think? The here-and-now is all that matters, the money we jingle in our pockets, the possessions we put around us, the security we think we find in all that. We don't think about eternity or talk about death. But we—who know Christ as our Saviour, the Lord, the Grain of wheat who fell into the ground and died and bore fruit of a living hope through His resurrection—have a hope which covers all that

miserable past of hopelessness and leads us into a glorious
future. You say how impossible it seems that a caterpillar
grub could possibly grow beautiful coloured wings and fly.
It's an impossibility! But it's true. And you say 'How can it
possibly be that earth-bound as we are, we can have a future
absolutely out of all proportion in our thinking to what we
now know?'

I want to say, with my hand on my heart, 'By faith in Jesus
Christ and the truth of His resurrection, that is true too. We
have a living hope through the resurrection of Jesus Christ
from the dead.'

Let me try and summarise then what Peter is saying, under
two headings, which I will put in the reverse order to Peter's.

The cross of Jesus

The cross of Jesus redeems me from all the failure of my past.
You've heard that so many times; hear it again and apply it to
your life. It's the fruit of the Grain of wheat that fell into the
ground on Calvary. The cross of Jesus redeems me from all
the failure of the past. Verse 18: 'You know that you were
ransomed from the futile ways inherited from your fathers,
not with perishable things such as silver or gold, but with the
precious blood of Christ, like that of a lamb without blemish
or spot.'

Ransom is a graphic word. We understand it instantly.
The kidnapped hostage cannot help himself. He is totally
dependent on another to buy his freedom for him. He's not
freed till the last penny is paid. Some theologians have
objected to some aspects of the analogy, but take it just as far
as Peter intended it to go. It's a graphic way of saying that
you and I are free from all the past. 'Not with perishable
things like silver and gold.' If you could pile up all the silver
and gold that this world possesses, it couldn't ransom you
from sin. But the precious blood of Christ as a lamb without
spot or blemish sets you free! There's hope for sinners.

The reference is of course to the Passover lamb, when the
children of Israel were redeemed from bondage in Egypt by
that last, dreadful plague when the firstborn were all killed—
save only in those homes where the blood of the lamb was

sprinkled on the lintel and door-posts of the home. Where the blood was sprinkled, where the lamb had been slain, as the night wore on and the appalling carnage went on through the land, in those homes and in those alone there was hope.

Immediately we must add, it was not the sort of indefinite hope that says 'Keep your fingers crossed.' Scripture unashamedly speaks of 'the full assurance of hope' (Heb. 6:11). That clashes with our normal usage, doesn't it, because hope for us implies uncertainty. But hope in Scripture has a full assurance. So those first-born of the Children of Israel, waiting through that long night as the destroying angel passed over the land, were not shivering in a vague unfounded hope that everything would turn out all right—the blood was there upon the lintel and doorposts of their homes. The lamb that had died had brought them hope in their darkness, a fully assured hope.

A little later in that same chapter the writer speaks of hope as like an anchor, sure and steadfast, for the soul. It's a lovely picture. This hope is a fruit of the Grain that died in the ground. We are ransomed by the blood shed on Calvary. The cross of Jesus, and that alone, redeems me from all the failure of my past. And through Him (1 Pet. 1:21) I have confidence in God, so that my faith is set firmly in Him.

I wonder if you've heard that so often that you need to hear it again tonight. The truth is, my dear brothers and sisters, there are Christians (including elderly Christians like me and some of you) whom Satan gets at in a particularly nasty way by trying to drag his filthy hands over the miserable failures of your past; to build up, if he can, an inhibiting guilt complex. Sometimes we older Christians—and younger ones too, I'm sure—fall for that kind of thing. And we wonder whether we really are saved. 'Can God forgive a sinner like me?'

'You don't know my past,' we ministers are often told. And I have to say 'No I don't, but I know one who does, and because of what He did on the cross when that Grain of wheat fell into the ground and died, a glorious hope broke into the darkness of the failure of your past and blotted it out all together. And that hope shines despite what Satan may in malice say; because that redemption is full, complete and perfect.' And as Peter says (verse 21), 'Through him you have confidence'—not doubts—'in God...because your faith and hope is in God.'

Let Him take you then, and discard all the insinuating doubts that Satan tries to place in your way. You have hope in Christ and in His finished work; and applied to your life it means that He's forgotten all about the past. It's forgiven, forgotten. You have a glorious living hope which covers all that's past.

The resurrection of Jesus

The cross alone redeems me from all the failure of my past. Now the resurrection of Jesus opens for me all the glory of His future (verse 3). By His death He has destroyed death and him who has the power of death, says Scripture—even Satan (cf. Heb. 2:14). And by His resurrection, His triumph on the cross over sin and death, and His resurrection—the glorious Easter-morning of that triumph—He blazes a trail to glory and says 'Come, follow Me!'

We have a living hope therefore through the resurrection of Jesus Christ from the dead, which takes us not just into tomorrow, next year and the year after that (though thank God it does that too) but a living hope that transforms our dying—an experience none of us has had, but which, unless He comes before we go, everyone of us will have. A hope that we as Christians can stand tall and face death, because through His dying and being raised to life we have a living hope which takes us all the pilgrim journey through—and, glory of glories! through death, into all that lies beyond.

It's only the Christian who can speak like that. It's only we who can stand up and talk unashamedly and uninhibitedly about dying. None of us has been there. There are uncertainties. But because He has been there and has triumphed over death and gone on through resurrection and ascension into glory, He says, 'This is the way! Follow Me! And all who will follow Me will go through death into resurrection and into glory, a living hope through the resurrection of the dead.'

Peter calls it (verse 4) an inheritance 'which is imperishable'. That means, beyond the reach of anything that death can do to it. The word 'perish' is the word Scripture uses about dying. But this glorious hope set before us is imperishable, an inheritance which death cannot touch. It's everlasting life. It's undefiled, he says. Everything down here, even the best we do for the Lord as Christians, is defiled by the touch of sin. Even the very handling of these pure pages of Scripture leaves our dirty finger marks upon it. God have mercy on us.

But in the Glory, there's no more sin. Isn't that *wonderful*? It's undefiled and never will be defiled, because sin will be a thing of the past. It's unfading beyond the reach of decay.

It's what Scripture calls the weight of glory. Isn't that a lovely expression? You see, the weight of money in your pocket is just nothing, it just fades and is gone. Yet what we so often think of as ethereal and weightless—Scripture says, 'Oh no, that's where real weight is, the weight of glory, unfading.' How beautiful that Old Testament verse is which Paul quotes: 'No eye has seen, nor ear heard, nor the heart of man conceived, what God has prepared for those who love him' (1 Cor. 2:9). We are born again to a living hope through the resurrection of Jesus.

So, verse 13, 'gird up your minds'. Think it through, for these transforming truths will change your way of life now and give new vigour to your step. Gird up your minds, think hard, get hold of these truths, vital to the well being of your Christian life. 'Gird up your minds, be sober, set your hope fully upon the grace that is coming to you at the revelation of Jesus Christ.'

I want to close with an illustration, a true story which is so awful that they'll never ask me to speak here again.

Last year we were living in a vicarage in Norwich. One day the sewers (this is the awful bit) got bunged up. It wasn't very nice. We called in a plumber, and he opened up the manhole. Ugh! What a sight! Then he asked to see the next manhole, and opened that. Ugh! What a stench!

He said, 'You go into the house and turn all the taps on and let them run. I'll poke around down here.' So we did. I watched him poke until suddenly, thank God, there was a horrible, sludgy, slimy noise and it all started to move, until—joy of joys!—pure clean water from the taps in the house came through the sewer. 'Thank you,' I said to the plumber, 'it's wonderful.'

I was about to pay him when he looked back into the manhole and said 'Is this yours?' And with his stick he retrieved a ring and washed it in a bucket. I said, 'It's probably out of a cracker.'

'I don't think so,' he said.

It was, if I remember correctly, two diamonds and a sapphire. I said, 'Well it's not mine, it's not my wife's—it might be one of our daughters' or daughters-in-law's, I'll ring them up and see.' But it wasn't theirs. 'Well, who's been to the vicarage in the last six months? We'd better find out.' We rang one or two people, but nobody claimed it. Is there anybody in this tent who's lost a ring? . . .

Isn't that a picture of some of us? You've been redeemed, not with silver and gold but with the precious blood of Christ. What are you doing, in what I can only call the sewers of your doubts and sins? *That's not where you belong.* By a miracle of God you've had your feet taken out of the mud, as the Psalmist says, and set on the rock; and your way has been established (Psa. 40:2). What are you doing down there? Gird up your minds.

If this applies to anybody here tonight, if you're a backslidden Christian dabbling in the sewers of sinfulness—God have mercy upon you, that's not where you belong. The fruit of that lovely Grain of the life of Christ fell into the ground and died there so that you might be redeemed from that. Come out! You don't belong there. Have done with that background of sin; stand for Christ, and let the hope for which He died at such cost burst in upon your sinfulness. What a challenge to us tonight! For the cross of Christ applies to everyone of us, for there's not one of us here who does not have to hang his head in shame and say, 'Oh God have mercy upon me the sinner.'

And just as that ring was made at such cost for the finger of some pretty girl somewhere in this kingdom, so God wants you for a glorious future—can I put it like this?—on His hand, to be with Him in that close relationship for all the days of your life here below, and on into eternity for ever with the Lord, Amen! So let it be.

Brother, sister, lift your eyes. Have done with the murkiness of being conformed to this world. Set your confidence in God, and know what it is to have a living hope through the resurrection of Jesus Christ. And come back to Him tonight if you need to, in true repentance and true faith. It was for this that the Grain of wheat died: that it might bring fruit in terms of lives transformed, and that those lives in turn might themselves bring forth fruit.

Note

1. Copyright © 1991 Richard Candlin. Reproduced by permission. This poem is part of a collection, *Go To The Ant*, which, it is hoped, will be published shortly.

'THE SPIRIT WHO GIVES LIFE'

by Mr Jonathan Lamb

Ezekiel 36:22–37:23

As we come to think about the Holy Spirit and His ministry, I'd like to begin by reading to you some wise but simple words from a few centuries ago, by Thomas à Kempis. Some of you will know them; they are from the first chapter of his classic *The Imitation of Christ*.

> What will it avail thee to dispute profoundly of the Trinity if thou be devoid of humility and art thereby displeasing to the Trinity?

Forty years ago the person and the work of the Spirit were neglected themes in our churches; with the possible exception of the Wesleyan and this Keswick tradition, few spoke of His ministry. But today there are acres of books, miles of ministry cassettes and weeks of conferences annually, all about the Holy Spirit. And while we can be deeply thankful for the enrichment that this emphasis has brought to the contemporary church world-wide, many of us are also saddened that during recent years the Holy Spirit has been the subject of so much division and bitterness and even spiritual pride.

Part of the problem has probably been that we've been looking at a doctrine rather than a Person. As David Watson used to say, 'The way we approach a proposition and the way we approach a person are two very different things, especially when that person is God.' And we might think that having defined the Holy Spirit's work with a set of neat doctrinal phrases, we somehow control Him. That is like climbing Skiddaw with a jam jar in your hand, trying to capture a gale-force wind! Perhaps we are in danger in forgetting that it is God Himself we are talking about, this all-powerful Creator, sustainer of the universe. And if we have a comfortable and domesticated view of the Holy Spirit we might forget that this God can and does break into human life in powerful and unexpected ways.

That was exactly Ezekiel's experience. Sometimes in the prophecy of Ezekiel the Holy Spirit is seen in almost physical terms. Several times He is described as 'lifting him up', as 'carrying him away'. In 37:1, 'He brought me out by the Spirit of the LORD and set me in a valley.' You see, we may pay lip-service to the Holy Spirit, but the question I have to ask this evening is whether or not we are taking seriously His powerful, unexpected ministry.

And I'd like to remind ourselves of three simple illustrations which this prophecy brings to us in chapters 36 and 37. The first is to do with hearts, the second with bones and the third with sticks. The first concerns the word from the Lord which Ezekiel prophesied concerning a radical change of heart; the second is the vision of revival which is familiar to us; and the third is a piece of street theatre which Ezekiel used to illustrate the restoration and unity of God's people. I have called the first,

Regeneration (36:24-27)

I read an article the other day by an evangelist. Its title was 'The heart of the human problem is the problem of the human heart.'

From the earliest days, as you know, God's relationship with Israel was described in terms of a covenant agreement. Basic to that agreement between God and His chosen people were certain requirements about their behaviour towards Him and each other. The covenant came with the assurance that they would be His people, they would receive His lesson. But there was a fatal flaw: the Israelites were obligated to obey, and yet time and again (as we know from the Old

Testament) they drifted away from their covenant responsibilities. They profaned God's name. And Ezekiel 36 has much to say about it.

So what could God do? He had two options. He could either reduce His demands, lower His standards so that they became within reach of His wayward people; or He could change their hearts. And Ezekiel and Jeremiah were given the task of prophesying to God's people that He was now going to keep both sides of the agreement. He would not only be faithful to His covenant agreement, but would also now equip them and empower them to keep their side of the bargain. Verse 26, 'a new heart'; verse 27, 'I will put my Spirit in you and move you to follow my decrees.' The term 'heart', as you probably know, really means the whole personality. God was promising them a radical psychological implant. It would be a complete change of heart so that now by God's Spirit people would be empowered to live as God intended them to live.

We know that this hope which Ezekiel proclaimed is a reality through Christ's work. What is it that stops you and me from living up to God's standards or even our own? It's not our environment, it's not our economic circumstances, it's not our family background—although all these things of course may aggravate the situation. It is, as Jesus was to say, internal. We need a radical change of heart. And the very beginning of the Christian's life and experience is to do with the Spirit's ministry of changing hearts. The heart of stone to which Ezekiel referred—that human will which is hostile to God, incapable of being changed for the better—is not beyond the transforming work of God's Holy Spirit.

I think that many people who are not Christians quite frequently miss this essential point about the Christian faith. I was talking to a test pilot not long ago. We were having a conversation about what it was that constituted being a Christian. I asked him: How does a person become a Christian? Almost without hesitation he said, 'It's a combination of indoctrination from environment, anxiety about the future, community pressures and awareness of moral obligations.' So I sat down and we began to talk about it.

Those phrases, as you unravel them, reveal the way that

many people think about the Christian faith: that it's all external, it's what you wear, it's what you say, it's the sort of church building you go into; it may be psychologically induced, it's brain-washing, it's things around you that influence you.

The apostle Paul gave very eloquent testimony. He said, 'However outwardly religious we may be, however much we may strive to attain God's standards we can never change what is the roots of the problem.' As he wrote to Titus: 'He saved us not on the basis of deeds which we have done in righteousness, but according to His mercy by the washing of regeneration and renewing by the Holy Spirit'—the two things Ezekiel mentions in verses 25-27—washing and the renewing by the Holy Spirit whom He poured out on us richly through Jesus Christ our Saviour. This is the regenerating work of the Holy Spirit who will touch hard hearts, open them, transform them, turn them to God and empower them to live as God intended us them live.

Many in this tent could testify to that regenerating work of the Spirit. Living as I do in the West Country, I love the story of William Haslam, the nineteenth-century vicar in Cornwall who was actually converted while preaching. This is what he says:

> I went into the pulpit and gave my text. I do not remember all I said but I felt a wonderful light and joy coming into my soul. Whether it was something in my words or my manner or my look I know not. All of a sudden a local preacher who happened to be in the congregation stood up and putting up his arms shouted out in the Cornish manner, 'The parson is converted, the parson is converted, Hallelujah.' And in another moment his voice was lost in the shouts and praises of three or four hundred in the congregation. Instead of rebuking this extraordinary bawling as I would have done in the former time, I joined in the outburst of praise. And to make it more orderly I gave out the doxology, 'Praise God from whom all blessings flow'.

It is this surprising, unexpected, powerful invasion of the Spirit, His regenerating work, which gives hope to all of us now engaged in the difficult task of bringing the gospel to our friends and our neighbours. You may have somebody in mind at this moment: a close friend, a spouse, a member of your family, maybe someone with whom you work. And you argue, you persuade, you explain, you appeal—these are all good categories for evangelism, but somehow you say to yourself, 'I cannot see him or her becoming a Christian.' Do you sometimes think that? But this passage and the New Testament says that the hardest heart is not beyond the reach of this life-giving Spirit. Don't ever give up praying for such a person!

And if that Holy Spirit has carried out the work of regeneration in your life and in mine by making us new, then that same Spirit will strengthen us to live lives according to God's law and standards. If you are involved in pastoral ministry or working with Christians you sometimes hear—maybe your friends or even you have said it yourself—a despairing Christian who says 'I cannot keep it up.' They feel paralysed by persistent failure and habitual sin. And they live with that tension that Paul knew—'I long to be like Christ and yet I feel pulled down by my sinful desires.'

Well, this passage speaks hope. God Himself is that hope by the Holy Spirit to will and to do His good pleasure. As Paul explains in that wonderful balance, 'If by the Spirit you put to death the misdeeds of the body you will live' (Rom. 8:13).

Changed hearts, regeneration.

Revival (37:1-14)

It's important to know Ezekiel's situation when the Lord gave him this picture. He lived in exile with God's people, hundreds of miles away from Jerusalem. There they were in the desert wastes of Babylonia; they'd received the news that Jerusalem, the city and the temple had been destroyed; now, away in exile, they had lost all hope. Despair had set in.

In this vision Ezekiel looks across this desert plain and sees an awful sight. It is the wreckage of a battle field. Nothing is left to interest even a starving vulture—a vast army of dead men's bones lying dismembered, dry as dust. And it's as if the Lord says to Ezekiel 'Well, Ezekiel, does this remind you of anything?' And Ezekiel says 'Yes Lord; it reminds me of my people.' He'd been prophesying a change in their fortunes, the possibility of changed hearts, new leadership, a restored land. But as his listeners heard his bold promises they thought it was simply false comfort. They looked at the scattered remains of the people in exile and they were completely sceptical. Can these bones live? They'd been in exile for about ten years and the bones were very dry indeed. All hope was lost.

So to verse 4. First of all Ezekiel was told to prophesy to the bones, 'Dry bones, hear the word of the Lord!' In this passage we find the words 'Spirit', 'breath' and 'wind'. They are all in fact translations of the same Hebrew word. As Ezekiel prophesied, there was a rattling sound and miraculously the bones came together. Verse 8: flesh appeared, skin covered them. Still they were lifeless. There was no breath in them. So next Ezekiel had to prophesy to the wind (it's the same word, remember, as 'breath' and 'spirit'). He appealed, in verse 9, 'Come from the four winds, O breath, and breathe into these slain, that they may live... and breath entered them; they came to life and stood up on their feet—a vast army.'

First and foremost this passage is a prediction of the way in which Israel as a nation would be reintegrated in their national, their political life. But I think we see in it immediately some very simple lessons for us and for our churches, because it doesn't take much imagination to see the state of the church and be so often reminded of the scattered dry bones rather than a living army.

The significant thing about this vision, you see, is that it emphasises again and again: it is God's work. Revival, bringing these bones back to life, shaping them into an army, is God's work. Ezekiel has simply followed instructions—'I prophesied as I was commanded.' If we are seeking revival within our own congregations we can't manufacture it. We can't organise it. Only God's Holy Spirit can bring that reviving power. Sometimes certain traditions advertise their meetings: at 6.30 pm there will be a revival meeting. But it can't be time-tabled like that. It is to do with God's sovereign, invading Spirit. And perhaps we can conclude from the two stages in the prophecy—proclaiming the word and then the Spirit of God breathing life—that if spiritual revival is to come to us and to the British churches and churches around the world which we represent this evening, it must at the very least have these twin components. It must have the word and the Spirit, the two things which we should never, ever, divorce. Throughout Christian history people have emphasised one or the other; but this prophecy in Ezekiel reminds us that God's reviving power will come through His word, faithfulness to the word and committed prayer for the Spirit's life-giving work.

Let me ask you, what sort of longing for spirituality do you have? Do you sometimes feel the awful sterility of a dry evangelical orthodoxy? There is such a thing. Do we seem to know little of God's work among us, with our structures, our committees, our programmes all appearing like dry bones?

Jim Packer wrote some interesting words while reading through 1 Corinthians 12-14. Whatever evils these chapters may confront us with, they show us a church in which the Holy Spirit was working with power.

> Reading them makes one painfully aware of the degree of impoverishment and inertia that prevails in churches today. If our reaction as readers is merely to preen ourselves and feel glad because our churches are free from Corinthian disorders we are fools indeed. The Corinthian disorders were due to an uncontrolled overflow of Holy Spirit's life. Many churches today are orderly simply because they are asleep, and with some one fears it is the sleep of death. It is no great thing to have order in a cemetery.

My brothers and sisters, I think the lesson of these verses is that the wind will blow through our churches and through our lives in response to prayerful obedience.

Jonathan Edwards, that great theologian of revival, says that when God has something very great to accomplish for His church it is His will that there should precede it the extraordinary prayers of His people. Nothing will happen in our churches until we are committed to that word and that Spirit, and with prayerful obedience are committed to seek Him to do that: 'Restore, oh Lord, the honour of Your name.' That's what the Lord promised: 'Once again I will yield to the plea of the house of Israel and do this for them'

(36:37). Revival—the Spirit who gives life! He can do it in our churches.

Let me finally point you to the third illustration.

Restoration (37:15-28)

Many of us stop reading after that story of the dry bones. But the chapter goes on. Very often Ezekiel would perform a piece of drama, a piece of street theatre to demonstrate something important; and here in verses 15-17 he brings a symbolic act to describe another phase of Israel's restoration.

Ezekiel's two sticks represented the two parts of the nation which had been divided ever since Solomon's time. Placing them end to end and holding them in his hand as a unity had a clear meaning. From being two nations, now they were one nation held together in God's hand. That was going to be God's purpose. The old divisions were being abolished, the nation would become united.

I want to emphasise one simple and most obvious point. God's purpose by the Holy Spirit is to unite His people. The Holy Spirit establishes the church, lives within the church, unites the church. Sometimes in talking about the Spirit's ministry we can be very individualistic. But the New Testament emphasis is quite frequently corporate. 'For we were all baptised by one Spirit into one body' (1 Cor. 12:13). You are being built together into a dwelling of God in the Spirit. 1 Corinthians 3:16—we sometimes think of this individualistically but it is to do with us as God's people too—'Don't you know that you yourselves are God's temple and that God's Spirit lives in you?'

In these days of institutionalised Christianity, it is exhilarating to see the church as a spiritual house of living people. It is living stones indwelt by the Spirit. Ezekiel saw that too. Look at the final verses of the chapter: 'My dwelling place will be with them; I will be their God, and they will be my people. Then the nations will know that I the Lord make Israel holy, when my sanctuary is among them for ever' (37:27-28).

Let me say one thing gently. This banner above me over the platform—'All one in Christ Jesus'—is not only a banner headline for Keswick. It is a spiritual reality and it should be a visible reality too. God's longing is that by the Spirit we should demonstrate unity. It would not surprise me if over fifty percent of us in this tent will return to local churches which are being almost torn apart by all sorts of division, whether it's personality clashes, disagreement over secondary doctrinal issues, even disapproval of the hymn book or the colour of the walls. Doesn't it happen? We need the Spirit's ministry, brothers and sisters.

A short while ago a friend of ours came back from taking her driving test. She said that she had unfortunately had some difficulty selecting second gear on a hill. The examiner was sitting in the seat next to her, watching her very carefully with his clipboard and biro at the ready as she struggled to select the gear. And finally as she struggled he said, 'Don't worry love, they're all in the same box, all you've got to do is sort them out.' That's a driving instructor with a ministry of encouragement! But you see that's exactly what Paul says to us. It's the New Testament stress on the New Testament church. We are all in the same family, we all belong to the one Father, we have all been redeemed by the one Lord Jesus Christ. We are all indwelt by the one Holy Spirit. Everything about your faith is one, Paul says in Ephesians 4. How can you possibly live in division? 'Make every effort to keep the unity of the Spirit through the bond of peace. There is one body and one Spirit' (Eph. 4:3-4).

And the Spirit's ministry among us and the congregations to which we return is not to iron out the differences into some bland uniformity. I'd like you to listen very carefully to my closing words. There is a doctrine that's much neglected among evangelicals. It's called the doctrine of difference. It's a New Testament doctrine we don't give much time to: it demands the ability to live with differences in our fellowships and still enjoy true mature Christian fellowship.

The Holy Spirit is not going to cover up all these differences. Instead He will give us the ability to live with them and enjoy true fellowship, true union, true reconciliation. And I believe that what we most urgently need from the Holy Spirit, when evangelicals are in danger of splintering in all sorts of ways and when our churches are in danger of echoing the fracture which we see in our own society, is that ministry of the Holy Spirit to unite and reconcile His people.

Working out that sort of unity in our churches is far less spectacular than other ministries of the Spirit. But I tell you, it is truly a sign and wonder when God's people demonstrate visible unity in the power of the Spirit. That is the essence of church life back home: fellowship in the Spirit.

Well, I conclude. Hearts, bones, sticks. Regeneration, revival, restoration. And tonight, brothers and sisters, let us seek God's Holy Spirit to soften hard hearts and empower us to live for Christ; to transform dry bones and to make us into a living army and to help us to stick together.

'PEOPLE IN GLASS HOUSES'

by Rev. Philip Hacking

John 8

Monday night in the Keswick Convention week is the night when we face the tremendous challenge of sin in the life of the believer. If we didn't start here, the week would be meaningless. Jesus began by preaching repentance, so did John the Baptist, so did Peter, so did Paul. So Monday always has a solemnity. And I want to preach on this Monday night, with God's help and your willing listening, from John's Gospel chapter 8—the well-known story of the woman taken in adultery.

You may be aware that we're not actually sure where this story should come in Scripture: one of the older manuscripts for example puts it Luke 21, with the Mount of Olives being the link. It needs a kind of theological detective to decide where it should come in the text. But I think nobody seriously doubts that this is authentic Jesus. It has all the marks of the Jesus of the Gospels, full of grace and truth. It's a remarkable story; and I would dare humbly this evening to try to make it relevant, if I can and need to, to all of us today.

Our Lord's religious attitudes very often clashed with those of the religious people of His day. In Mark 7, for example, Jesus and the Pharisees had a great argument about what made a person unclean. The Pharisees reckoned if you touched something unclean, if you mixed with Gentiles and unclean people, you made yourself unclean. Jesus said no, it's what comes out of a man that makes him unclean. It's the heart of man that needs to be changed. And here is the tremendous message of Keswick. Even on a Monday night the joy is that it's not a miserable night. We live on the other side of the cross. We can have a new heart.

Well do I remember years ago when I was ministering at Edinburgh. It was New Year's Day. As you know if you are a Scot, nobody gets up on New Year's morning. New Year's Day doesn't exist, it merges into the day before. And on New Year's Day 1968 I was lying in bed listening to the news headlines. The first item was the report that the great South African doctor Dr Christiaan Barnard had performed what I think was the first publicised heart transplant operation. It was great news and we rejoiced. It seemed, and still does, a miracle to those of us who don't understand medicine—that you could give a man a new heart.

The second item reported that the truce in Vietnam had ended and they were slaughtering each other again. And I said to myself—preachers are always thinking of sermons, even in bed on New Year's morning—what a sermon; you can give somebody a new heart physically, but you cannot— apart from God the Spirit—give somebody a new heart spiritually, to change him from within. Thank God we can! And Keswick of course stands for that message. But it will only be relevant when we recognise that we need a new heart. That's what makes us unclean.

Ask yourself this question. Suppose you'd been there that day. Be honest, whose side would you have been on? Jesus— or the Pharisees? Where do you think you would have been? Let me tell you one other thing, because this sermon can only be meaningful if you accept it, that nowhere in Scripture, least of all in the New Testament, do you sit in an armchair viewing. You're in the dock, and so am I. It's always God speaking to me. And I shall only be content tonight if every single one of us tonight is listening. It's not, 'Who is God speaking to tonight?' but 'What is God saying to me tonight?'

Let me put this in context. In the world in which we live— and Keswick must always be earthed in the world in which we live, as well as in the eternal unchanging word—we're living in an age where everybody outside of Christ says that things are relative. 'You can believe what you like—if it's true for you it's true.' There is nothing that is objectively wrong. If it's right for you, fine. And that world in which we live begins to seep into the church. Think about it another way. Because, thankfully, in some of our churches we are beginning to move out into that world, and particularly when you begin to move into the world of the teenagers and those in their twenties today, you begin to come into a world where people have been infected with all these concepts.

How should the church react?

There are two dangers. One is that we begin to forget our landmarks, we begin to move the goalposts. Because it's hard to say these judgemental things, we begin to say, 'Well of course, it doesn't matter today. We can change our views.' The other danger is that we're *only* judgemental. With the Pharisees, we cast stones. I've called this talk 'People in glass houses'—and you know how it goes on, don't you.

As we move into that world we're moving into a world where we're challenged by what Paul calls in Galatians 5 'the works of the flesh'. And I wonder if you've ever noticed, there are fifteen illustrations of the works of the flesh. May I remind you, so that we can set the scene, just what those fifteen are? The first three are sexual sins. Make no mistake about it, they are sins. Nowhere in this story did Jesus suggest that they do not matter. He did not say, 'Neither do I condemn you.' It is almost an insult to the Almighty to say that His Son actually said to a woman taken in adultery *only* 'Neither do I condemn you.' Neither do I condemn you—*go and sin no more.*' That makes all the difference in the world to what He had to say.

I want to suggest to some of you that we need to listen very carefully to these sexual sins. There are three of them there in Galatians 5. I would be very surprised if there are not some people here in this tent tonight who need to come clean with God. I now meet people who want to say to me that living together is quite reasonable and acceptable, that it's actually a good way of preparing yourself for marriage. I read that these young people—and not only young people—have a kind of commitment. Can I say to you quite straightforwardly, that if you live together outside marriage you are clearly condemned by the word of Scripture; it comes in this category of sexual sin. What's more, your chance of being divorced is twice as high as if you did not live together before marriage. Can we kill the idea that it actually makes people more able to live together? Statistics published last week show that more than twice as many people get divorced who live together before marriage than who do not. And in this gathering tonight there may well be some who in their heart of hearts know that this is where they are.

The next two are sins to do with the occult and witchcraft. Oh, we all abhor those! The funny thing is that sometimes we abhor things and yet begin to become fascinated by them on the edges of our thinking. And I believe that some kinds of so-called Christian religions get very near the occult.

The last two works of the flesh are to do with drunkenness. Isn't it interesting how in recent years—rightly, I think— we've been liberated from a foolish negativism on this matter of alcohol? But have you noticed, when people are emancipated or think they're emancipated, they become very critical of those who are not! I believe we need to be very careful about how lightly we treat alcohol. It's a very real problem, it's a growing problem.

That's seven out of the fifteen. What are the other eight? Let me read some of them to you. 'Hatred, jealousy, selfish ambition, factions, envy'—and if you want me as a parish minister to be straight down the line as far as sexual sins are concerned, by all means: but I hope you won't mind if I'm as straight down the line when it comes to envy and pride and selfish ambition. On what grounds do you want me to ostracise the sexual sinners and to smile sweetly on those who hate their fellow Christians, who are envious of position?

So I come back to this story. There are three pictures here in John chapter 8. I see first of all condemnation at work. I then see conscience at work. And finally I see compassion at work.

Condemnation at work (8:1-6)

There's a contrast between verse 2 (true religion) and verses 3-6 (counterfeit religion). It's easy to miss verse 2. It seems very ordinary. At dawn He appeared again in the temple courts and He sat down to teach when the people gathered round him. That's just setting the scene, surely? No. That's real religion. That's the heart of true Christian ministry. That's the answer to the problems of our day. That's where we're going to see things change. If we teach the word of God, then sin will be called sin and forgiveness will always be there.

Have you noticed how often Jesus taught and things happened? When four friends broke open a roof and lowered their paralysed friend to the feet of Jesus—we all know that story—do you realise what the context was? Loads of people, no doubt hundreds, swarming round the house listening to Jesus teaching. Although the life of that one man was important, do remember it was in the context of the ministry of Jesus teaching.

The feeding of the five thousand—so misunderstood. They weren't starving like those tragic people we see on our television screens. They were hungry, but they could easily have gone home to get food. They weren't going to die. Why did He feed them? Because they were so busy listening to God's word they forgot about their physical needs. The crowds were gathered to listen to Jesus teaching.

Do you know, I think the first sin in the life of a believer to be confessed tonight by some ministers and teachers here is that we've lost out on making the word of God central. Paul says in 2 Corinthians 4:2 that he sets forth the truth plainly. It's my deep desire as a minister to do that more. It's important if I believe it's the truth, to make it plain to people. It's important that I do not get distracted from it, whatever other people may say. And may I say, you who are not ministers, encourage your minister to make that word central. Do you gather when he wants to expound it in your church? When you have groups in your home, what's at the centre? Do you sit around and 'share'? That has its place. But do you sit around God's word? The sin of the church today may well be that we've lost confidence in the word of God, and the moral slide in the world is in many ways the fault of the church. The challenge comes to us.

I commend to you *The Church that Turned the World Upside Down*, by Roy Clements who gave splendid Bible Readings here last year.[1] I wrote a foreword, and when I got the proofs they'd actually put the heading incorrectly as 'The Church Turned Upside Down'. I thought it was a jolly good title, if accidental. For I believe it's when the church is turned upside down that the world will get turned upside down, and that we shall begin to make inroads into today's world, with all its problems, when the church has the word of God central. When God's word is at work, there is a real risk that our lives may turn upside down. But there is little risk if we sing the nice choruses we all like singing, gather around to hear the kind of things we like hearing, and aren't challenged by the word.

What is counterfeit religion? (8:3-6a)

I hope you are listening carefully, because I don't want people to accuse me of what I've not said. It is a thin tightrope I'm walking tonight. If I fall off, forgive me. What was our Lord's attitude, when they brought this woman taken in adultery; was He saying it didn't matter?

Let's go back to John 3 and 4 where Jesus talked to two very different people. In 2:25 we're told that Jesus knew what was in man. There follows in 3:1-21 the story of Nicodemus. He told Nicodemus—remember?—'You must be born again.' In chapter 4 He meets a woman, the exact opposite; a woman incidentally who was living with a man who was not her husband. He didn't pretend it didn't matter. He made it abundantly clear, as He pointed out that woman's sin. But He said to her, 'God is Spirit, and his worshippers must worship in Spirit and in truth' (4:24).

Now if I'd been clever enough to have thought up those two statements, I'd have said to Nicodemus 'God is Spirit' and we'd have had a debate about the person of God; and I'd have said to the woman at the well, 'You must be born again'. Jesus unerringly got it the other way round. You see, those Pharisees who'd brought this woman in John 8 needed to be born again. There are many religious people who have very high concern about moral integrity who still desperately need to be born again. And the woman who had been taken in adultery and the woman at the well who knew she was a sinner needed to know—yes, of course they had to be born again, but they needed to know that there was hope that Jesus loved and Jesus cared.

The Pharisees brought a woman. She had sinned: the law said she had to be stoned. Have you noticed one or two things? I hope I'm not being pedantic—but where was the man? It says they caught her in the act of adultery, so presumably the man was caught as well; and the Bible makes it absolutely clear that both man and woman should be taken. And will you notice in verse 6, that they were doing it deliberately as a trap to catch out Jesus, just as they did when they asked about whether they should pay the tax to Caesar or not? Do you see what's happened? They had condemned the woman already, they had added one sin to another, she was a sinner but their sin was a sin of utter carelessness— harsh legalism, no love, no care.

Of course the law still matters. You remember Matthew 5:17, where Jesus said, 'I have not come to abolish the Law but to fulfil it. I tell you the truth'—here's our law, the Sermon on the Mount—'until heaven and earth disappear, not the smallest letter, not the least stroke of a pen, will by any means disappear from the Law until everything is accomplished.' Jesus is saying here that the law does matter; what the Old Testament says is desperately important. Our Lord doesn't deny it. But here were the Pharisees, concerned only to catch Jesus out. They cared nothing for the woman. Friends—do you? Of course you do. But do you have to minister sometimes to people who are going through this or similar troubles? If you have no heart of love, stay away. Don't meddle in counselling. Without a heart of love you have no right to say anything.

The tragedy of these counterfeit religious people is that they were one or other of two extremes. Either they condemned without offering help, or they said 'Peace, peace' when there was no peace. Any kind of religion can be evaluated by the place it gives to the cross. If you only condemn, what about the cross? Did He not die for that woman caught in adultery? And if you say of course it doesn't matter now, everything's all right, it's all relative today—then again you dismiss the cross. There's no need for it if we all get to heaven in any case.

To me, their tragedy is that they thought they were all right. There was nothing for them in this message. Wasn't that the rich young ruler who, when Jesus challenged him, said of the Law, 'All this have I kept from my youth'? Wasn't it Saul before he was converted who thought he was all right because he kept the letter of the law? There is condemnation at work. And I wonder whether some of us are still there.

Conscience at work (8:6-9b)

We move on. We notice first of all the sword of the word, verses 6b and 8. Now here's where commentators divide into two groups. There are those who think that Jesus wrote some very telling words—a message; the crowd were given a visual sign in the sand. We don't know what He said, of course, but they were powerful words. And there are those who think He was just doodling, just like I do during long telephone calls. I think He was doodling. He was waiting for conscience to have its work.

Jesus didn't answer their question. In a sense they had Him where they wanted Him. If He said they shouldn't condemn the woman He was not keeping the law of Moses. If He said they should follow the law of Rome, which forbade capital punishment for religious offences, He would be in trouble too. So He didn't answer. What did He do?

Please note this. He said, 'If anybody is without sin let him cast the first stone.' You see? He's actually trying to bring these Pharisees to the place of repentance for their sin. He's saying to the Pharisees, 'Forget the woman. What about your sin?' And I love how in Scripture it's always the way with the great people. Paul, on trial for his life, standing in front of King Agrippa. He's supposed to be defending himself; but he comes to the point where he says to Agrippa, 'You believe the Scriptures don't you?' King Agrippa says, 'Are you trying to make me a Christian?' and Paul says, 'I would that you were exactly as I am, apart from these chains.' He was making a great gospel appeal. Standing before Felix who loved to ask him awkward questions, He began to talk about righteousness, self-control and judgement to come. Felix didn't like that one little bit. But Paul was trying to bring him to repentance and faith.

And here is the challenge of Jesus: 'He who is without sin, cast the first stone.' May I just say, in passing, that this does not mean that sinners cannot judge others? I have a very delightful judge in my congregation. But if he were only allowed to judge people if he were himself sinless, he couldn't do it. Nobody could. No: what is being said is this. How dare you try to take the mote out of your brother's eye, if you haven't taken the beam out of your own?

Was Jesus was referring to the sin of adultery? I wonder. I don't think He was saying, 'If anyone is without the sin of adultery let him cast the first stone'—though I would say to you that our Lord's words in Matthew 5:27-30, where He talks about the sin of adultery being sin in the mind and lusting in the heart, mean that many who condemn others are themselves condemned.

I remember Dr Martin Lloyd-Jones preaching at the time of a great parliamentary scandal. He asked the congregation, 'How many of you read every detail of that sordid story in the newspaper even while you were condemning it? All over this country at the moment there are thousands of people who are committing adultery by proxy.' I guarantee you could pick up this morning's paper and read some salacious stuff about scandal in high places. Do you read it? Why? Is there not a danger that God is saying to us 'Are you without even this sin?'

I believe our Lord is saying this. The one who can honestly stand up and say 'I am without sin' may condemn others. But only if you can say that. And who can?

May I remind you of that sad story of David, who wrote 'The Lord is my Shepherd' and sinned adulterously with Bathsheba? I think the worst bit of that story is when David, having committed adultery with Bathsheba, sends Uriah her husband to the front line with a note to the general telling him to be sure Uriah was killed. David knew that loyal Uriah would not even presume to look into a letter given him by the king. Can anybody stoop lower than David? And do you remember Nathan's courageous story, and David's angry verdict—'He shall die!' He pronounced judgement on himself. Nathan said, 'You are the man.'

Dare you, by the way you judge others, judge yourself? We shall get nowhere this week of Convention, unless first of all we put ourselves in the dock.

I don't find it easy to preach this kind of sermon, but preach it I must. But here's the hopeful note at the end. Just before we come to it, may I mention in passing that not only was the sword of the word at work but also but the power of the word (verse 9). Isn't it interesting? Conscience began to work. I'm always intrigued by the fact that they left in order of seniority. They kept their ritual right to the end. But what I do know that is that they all went out, all convicted. And I hope with all my heart that as we go out of this tent shortly we shall go out, all of us, convicted.

Compassion at work (8:10-11)

They didn't—they couldn't—condemn her. Our Lord was left alone with the woman. And here's the lovely balance of grace and truth.

He did say to her, 'Neither do I condemn you.' He could say it, because He was the only man who could condemn. 'Which of you convinces me of sin?' says verse 46. He was sinless and was made sin for us. He could have said 'I condemn you'; He had every right. And Jesus could preach condemnation. He could preach hell. There's no suggestion that He toned down God's standards. He could only say, 'Neither do I condemn you' because there would come a moment in a year or so's time when He would be hanging on that cross, bearing the sins of that woman, of those Pharisees, of the woman at the well, of Nicodemus; and all of them would, or could, kneel at the foot of the same cross. And Paul could cry 'There is now no condemnation to those who are in Christ Jesus' (Romans 8:1).

I love that hymn of Charles Wesley: 'No condemnation now I dread, Jesus and all in Him is mine.' But there is only no condemnation because He died and we are in Him. The church does not preach 'No condemnation' to the world. It preaches the Christ who died so that there might not be condemnation. The gospel is for penitent sinners. It's grace and truth. You see, He didn't just say 'Neither do I condemn you', He said 'Neither do I condemn you, *go now and leave your life of sin.*' Because Jesus forgave her, there was the motivation to live a new life. Paul could say, 'You're not your own, you're bought with a price, so glorify God in your body.'

One more story in John, to drive the message home. Do you remember the man in John 5 who'd been paralysed for thirty-eight years? I always remember this story because when I was a young curate aged twenty-four my vicar asked me, 'Will you go and visit this lady? She's been paralysed in bed for twenty-five years.'

I said, 'She's been in bed longer than I've been alive! What do I say to her?'

'Off you go—you'll do it,' said the vicar. And off I went. I went in to see that dear lady, I'll always remember her. She said to me, 'Oh, God is so good! I've so much to thank Him for.' Really? Twenty-five years on your back? And as it came to the point when I knew as a young curate I was supposed to pray, I thought—How do I pray for this lady? She must have recognised my problem, for she said, 'Would you like me to pray for you?' I said, 'Yes please.' She did. It was a lovely prayer, she saw my need was greater than hers and she prayed. A beautiful lady.

I think about her when I see this man in John 5 who'd been on his back, thirty-eight years paralysed. Jesus heals him, then in John 5:14 goes back to him and says, 'Don't sin any more, lest a worse thing happen to you.' What—worse than thirty-eight years on your back? Yes. Our Lord spoke solemnly about the awesomeness and the reality of hell. Thirty-eight years paralysed is nothing compared to that. And here is our Lord, trying to say to this man as he said to this woman: 'Don't sin any more, I've healed you, sir, so now live a new life; I've forgiven you, madam, so now go and live a new life.' I can't prove it, but I'm sure you and I will meet this woman eternity. I'm sure she did turn from sin, because she'd been much forgiven.

As I finish, let me read these very solemn words of Jesus from the Gospel of Matthew, addressing the same people. 'I tell you the truth, the tax collectors and the prostitutes are entering the kingdom of God ahead of you. For John came to you to show you the way of righteousness, and you did not believe him, but the tax collectors and the prostitutes did.

And even after you saw this you did not repent and believe him' (Matthew 21:32).

It is possible that some who are like this woman find it easier to kneel at the foot of the cross than some high-minded moral person who finds it so difficult to bow the knee. Sometimes the prostitutes do get there ahead of us. You remember the Pharisee in the story of Jesus, who stood and prayed with himself and thanked God that he wasn't like this publican? How right he was! 'This publican' was being converted. He was praying for forgiveness. How dare we judge ourselves by others. Not long ago in Northern Ireland I was told of a recently converted couple who were lapping up Bible teaching. And an older member of their congregation said to me: 'Isn't it funny? It's easier to get this couple come to a Bible Convention teaching week, than some of our regulars who've been church members for donkeys' years but don't seem to want to come and listen to the word of God.'

How sad. Our Lord went into a Pharisee's home and received no welcome. And a woman there, to whom the Pharisee wouldn't even talk, anointed Him and showed her love. Because she had been forgiven much, she loved much.

As we close, all of us need to respond. It's not for me to say how. Maybe there are people who are living together outside of marriage. Are you ready to repent? That's not saying sorry, it's stopping. And it can be done. There's no point in coming to the rest of the week to expect blessing if you will not repent at the level you know you ought. I've had more than one person sit in my study and say to me, 'I want this that and the other in my spiritual life,' and I've had to say to them, 'But you're living with somebody out of marriage, and until you stop that you can't expect anything else to happen. You're playing games with God. And He doesn't play games, ever. He is saying to you, "Go and sin no more." '

But I guess you are a very small minority here. Some of us need to come repenting of our judgmentalism, repenting of our lack of love; even while I've been preaching your mind has been thinking not of yourself and your sin but of others and theirs. Jesus asks you to respond to His love. He went to the cross because He loved that woman, and He loved those

Pharisees, and He loved Nicodemus, and He loved the woman at the well. And that love will never let you go. But you must respond to it.

Note

1. Roy Clements, *The Church that Turned the World Upside Down* (Crossway, 1992).

'THE SIGN OF THE CROSS'

by Rev. George Hoffman OBE

Earlier this year a group of us were discussing the carnage in Croatia, the slaughter in Somalia, and the latest victims of violence in Northern Ireland. And someone reminded us of the common factor in all three—the reality of primeval, unredeemed human nature.

In our conversation we were also reminded how this was reflected in William Golding's brilliant but brutal allegory, *Lord of the Flies*. It is the story of a group of young boys who are shipwrecked on a deserted island. Slowly their relationships disintegrate into feuding and the most appalling atrocities. And Golding chillingly describes their degeneration into tribalism and unadulterated brutality. Gradually one of the boys, Ralph, recognises the problem of their plight. He sees that they are unable to save themselves, that they need help from outside. Golding writes,

> 'If only they could get a message to us,' cried Ralph desperately. 'If only they could send us something grown-up...a sign or something.'

Tonight, to a world that echoes a similar desperation and despair, the cross of Calvary is that message—that sign, that something for that someone. 'When the time had fully come,' writes Paul in Galatians 4:4, 'God sent his Son, born of a woman, born under law, to redeem those under law, that we might receive the full rights of sons.'

Now, looking at what Christ accomplished on the cross it's important to understand both the nature of our sin and the nature of our salvation. You see, you and I are not sinners because we sin. A dog is not a dog because it barks, it barks because it's a dog. And you and I sin because we are sinners. Similarly, the reason our Lord's sacrifice for sin was accepted was not that He died on the cross; He sacrificed His life on the cross because He was sent to be our Saviour. What He accomplished on the cross was accepted by God because of who He was, not just because of what He did. 'There was none other good enough to pay the price of sin, He only could unlock the gate of Heaven and let us in.'

This is the basis of Paul's argument in the opening chapter of his little letter to the Colossians. Turn to it with me, as we focus in upon the cross. 'For he has rescued us from the dominion of darkness and brought us into the kingdom of the Son he loves, in whom we have redemption, the forgiveness of sins' (Col. 1:13). So first we are rescued by Christ; He has rescued us from the dominion of darkness. Secondly we are released by Christ, we are brought into the kingdom of the Son He loves. Thirdly, we are redeemed by Christ in whom we have redemption, the forgiveness of sins. And fourthly (verse 20) we are reconciled to God by Christ—'and through him to reconcile to himself all things, whether things on earth or things in heaven, by making peace through his blood, shed on the cross.'

There couldn't be a more forceful statement of substitutionary theology—the all-sufficient sacrifice because of the all-sufficient Saviour; ransomed, healed, restored, forgiven.

I've had the pleasure of sharing a platform with Derick Bingham before, both in Belfast as well as here at Keswick. Like most communicators, as you've guessed already, he has his fair share of favourite words. One of them is 'awesome'. Well, he may not know it but he's in good company, at least according to the Living Bible, because this is how that version translates Psalm 130:4, contemplating God's grace, mercy and love. The psalmist says this, 'But you forgive! What an awesome thing this is!' I think that's how John Newton must have felt when he penned the hymn, 'When I survey the wondrous cross, On which the prince of glory died, My richest gain I count but loss, And pour contempt on all my pride.' He had that sense of awesomeness.

Cliff Richard had to sing in a Moscow stadium soon after things loosened up while it was still within the Russian empire. He chose to sing that hymn at the end of the concert, and he decided to sing it unaccompanied in that vast stadium. You could have heard a pin drop. What you couldn't see at the end of the song were the tears trickling down his face. He said, 'I just felt it was so awesome. Not the place I was singing in but the person I was singing about.'

Have you noticed how already the theme for this year's Convention has been coming through in Derick's Bible Readings, right from the start? On Saturday evening he referred to King David's royal appointment.[1] But although David was acknowledged and approved, and although he was appointed and anointed before he wore that crown, like the King of Kings he prefigured David endured considerable conflict. Without the cross there is no crown.

Did you notice this morning and in yesterday's Bible Reading that although Esther was summoned to wear the crown, she also suffered under the cross? I don't think it's without significance that the theme for this year's Keswick Convention is, 'The cross and the crown'. You see, it's one of the basic facts of our faith, it's foundational, it's fundamental: without the cross there is no crown.

Wasn't that why Jesus had to rebuke Peter with those memorable words, 'Get thee behind me, Satan'? Why did He say that? Because He was tempted to take a short cut. And He knew that without the cross there is no crown. Wasn't that why Jesus spelt it out to the disciples on three separate occasions, with almost monotonous repetition? Mark 8, 'The Son of man must suffer many things.' Mark 9, 'The Son of man will be betrayed into the hands of men and they will kill him.' Mark 10, 'The Son of man will be mocked and spat on and flogged.' Without the cross there is no crown. That's why He steadfastly set His face towards Jerusalem. And He knew that before it became the place of enthronement, it would first become the place of execution.

In one of his books Paul Tournier has accurately summed up the modern mood that Dr Raymond Brown sees prevailing in society and in the church today. Listen to what Tournier says.

> We're nearly always longing for an easy religion, easy to understand, easy to follow, a religion with no mystery, no insoluble problems, no snags. A religion that would allow us to escape from our miserable human condition. A religion in which contact with God spares us all strife, all uncertainty, all suffering and all doubt. In short, a religion without the cross.

In his *Imitation of Christ* Thomas à Kempis writes, 'If indeed there had been anything better and more beneficial to man's salvation than suffering, Christ certainly would have shown it by word and by example. But He didn't because He couldn't.'

'There was none other good enough to pay the price of sin, He only could unlock the gate of Heaven and let us in.'

Over the years I've had to make a number of visits to South-East Asia and the borders of Cambodia and Laos, and visit many of the refugee camps in those places. Now the infamous railway crossing from Thailand to Burma has been opened for tourists on the fiftieth anniversary of its construction during the Second World War. It was built by prisoners of war. It became widely known through the film, *The Bridge on the River Kwai*, starring Sir Alec Guinness. But a far more meaningful record has been preserved of what happened on the Kwai railway in a little book by Ernest Gordon called *The Miracle on the River Kwai* (currently out of print). In it, the author—who served as an army chaplain among the prisoners—records the best and the worst of human nature and all that man is capable of doing to other men. Man's inhumanity to man, man's courage and compassion. There's one particular incident that reflects these qualities. Let me share it with you.

After the prisoners had returned from a day's digging, it was discovered that one of the shovels was missing. The camp guard commanded the guilty person to step forward. When no one moved the guard threatened that they would all be executed. 'All die, all die!' he screamed. At that moment, writes Ernest Gordon,

An Argyll soldier stepped forward, stood stiffly to attention and said calmly, 'I did it.' The guard unleashed all his whipped-up hate, he kicked the helpless prisoner and beat him with his fists and still the Argyll stood rigidly to attention. The blood was streaming down his face. His silence goaded the prison guard to an excess of rage. Seizing his rifle by the barrel he lifted it high over his head and with a final howl brought it down on the skull of the Argyll who sank limply to the ground and did not move. Although it was perfectly clear that he was dead, the guard continued to beat him and stopped only when exhausted. The men of the work detail picked up their tools. They picked up their comrade's body and they marched back to camp. When the tools were counted again at the guard house no shovel was missing. Greater love has no man than this, that a man lay down his life for his friends.

It's a graphic illustration of our Lord's own words and a graphic illustration of our Lord's own work and what He accomplished on that cross. A work that's summed up again in the well-known hymn, 'Bearing shame and scoffing rude, in my place condemned He stood; sealed my pardon with His blood—Hallelujah! what a Saviour.'

Very soon now the world's attention will be focused once again on the 1992 Olympics, at Barcelona. Originally the Greek word for the games was the *agon*. It's the word from which we derive our word in the English, 'agony'. At that time throughout the known world the contest was looked upon as the ultimate human achievement. All contestants were totally dedicated to it, totally devoted to it and totally disciplined in their pursuit of the *agon*, to win the crown of the games.

They considered the *agon*—the agony—was worth every drop of blood, every drop of sweat, every tear that was shed in order to obtain the crown. And so too did our Lord Jesus Christ. He was totally dedicated and devoted to His task. He was totally disciplined in the pursuit of it. He too considered the *agon*—the agony—worth every drop of blood, every drop of sweat, every tear that was shed in order to obtain the crown. There is just one difference. They did it, and still do, for their own benefit. But He did it for ours. He who knew no sin was made to endure sin, for people like you and me who enjoy sin. I stand before you tonight and say that I enjoy sin;

it's part of my sinful human nature. And I constantly repent of that sin and ask forgiveness for that sin.

But the Lord Jesus Christ was made sin for me who knew no sin, that I might become the righteousness of God in Him. He endured the sin that I enjoyed and endured the ultimate agony for it. 'My God, My God, why hast Thou forsaken Me?'

That's what I deserve. 'My God, my God, because of what I've done, why have You forsaken me?'

'George—I haven't! Because He's done all that's necessary for Me to forgive you, to accept you. You are accepted in My Beloved.'

As a young Christian I remember learning some of the basic ABC's of evangelism. A—Admit you're a sinner. B—Believe that Christ can save you. C—Count the cost of your commitment. Tonight, as we close, I want to count the cost of His commitment. Too often the emphasis is placed upon my cost. What about *His* cost? The Son of God who became the Son of man, so that the sons of men could become the sons of God—what a cost! I want to count the cost that He paid...the cost of the sacrifice that He made...the cost of the love that He displayed.

> Wounded for me, wounded for me,
> There on the cross, He was wounded for me.

And as a result,

> Gone my transgressions and now I am free,
> All because Jesus was wounded for me!
> ...
> Help me to understand it,
> Help me to take it in,
> What it meant for Thee, the Holy One,
> To take away my sin.

Note

1. This refers to an address not included in the present volume. The tape (no. 35) can be obtained from ICC at the address given on p. 219.

'WHO OWNS ME?'

by Mr Derick Bingham

Daniel 3:16-30

Almost everyone looks upon the Book of Daniel with a sense of wonder and great anticipation, because it is usually regarded both by theologians and believers as a book that foretells the future. There's a lot of prophecy in Daniel, and certainly if you want to know about God's programme for the future it is essential that you understand this book. God does not unfold to us all the details of the future that is coming in this world, any more than He unfolds the details of our own individual future. What He does show us is the general trend of events and where it will end. If you investigate this area you will discover significant and helpful things about what is happening in our world today. But one of the great problems with teaching and studying the Book of Daniel is the symbolic language that the Holy Spirit inspires Daniel to use. It is very difficult to understand. Very unusual things appear, especially animals, strange beasts with different heads and horns sticking out here and there and images of all kinds of indescribable visions.

Without question the Book of Daniel deals again and again with God's critique of world, national and local government. In Daniel 2 we find the amazing vision sent to Nebuchadnezzar and interpreted by Daniel as representing coming kingdoms of various kinds, of Greece and Rome and so on. His vision was of a great figure with a head of gold, arms of silver, belly of bronze—and feet of iron and clay.

When you consider it, it is clearly God giving him a vision of coming governments of the world in the likeness of a beautiful piece of art.

In Daniel 7 you get another critique of government by God, this time representing them as animals. Some say, 'But surely this is a contradiction—how can governments be both like a lovely art form and like animals?' Well, let me put it very simply.

If you were to invite a lion home for tea he wouldn't say 'Pass the salt and pepper'. If he was hungry he would have our heads off without please or thank you. Animals live according to their instincts and appetites. They are not governed by the kind of morality that human beings should be, and are, governed by, and against which they often fight. In the Scriptures we repeatedly read that God gets very angry with His people when He sees animals doing by instinct what we should be doing with our understanding. 'The swallow always comes back' says God, 'but My people never come back to Me, many of them' (cf. Jer. 8:7).

Throughout the Scriptures you see this image: 'The ox knows its owner...but Israel does not know, my people do not consider' (Isa. 1:3). That beautiful example of the birds of the air, too, 'who toil not neither do they spin' (Matt. 6:28)— it doesn't mean the little birds don't work, it means they don't toil like people do. But they work very hard building their nests, and they have accidents, they die of starvation and cold. Yet they are without anxious care. And we go around half the time with our stomachs like spin driers. We're frustrated, uptight and worried.

Sometimes I look upon the people of God and into my own heart and I say 'Do I really know the God of peace, are my sins forgiven? Am I on my way to glory? If I am, and Christ is Lord, then why am I so uptight and filled with worry?'

Yes, we can learn a lot from the animals. But they live by instinct. We have what the mule does not. God says 'Do not be like the horse or like the mule which have no understanding' (Psa. 32:9). You've been given understanding to understand and know the things of God. So whenever in the Book of Daniel you have governments likened to animals, God is saying 'Governments don't always behave as human people should behave.' We have seen Hitler, Stalin, Napoleon and Saddam Hussein arise, we have seen the warlords of Sarejevo hurling weapons against each other and breaking cease-fire agreements. The governments of the West have not always behaved with understanding; many will intervene only when their oil or other national interests are threatened. Governments have very often behaved like animals, even wiping out by genocide those that they don't want in their land. We think of six to eight million Jews wiped out by a government run by a dictator...

But then, the Scriptures show us, governments sometimes do behave like a lovely art form. Look at the fantastic roads built by the Romans, electricity and similar benefits in much of the modern world. Governments have often behaved very well, producing good projects and ideas. You can say they sometimes behave like a lovely art form, lovely in what they do, while at other times they can behave by instinct like animals.

But the teaching of the introduction to the Book of Daniel is, very simply, that no matter what form of government there is in the world, there has never been one that was perfect. The image that Nebuchadnezzar saw of government was that it was unstable—feet of clay indeed. There has never been a government in history that has been able to fulfil one hundred percent the promises it has made to its people. Only God delivers one hundred percent of His promises. They are 'Yea' and 'Amen' in Christ. Lean hard on them, Christian. They are certain and sure.

I hope that will be a little key as to what is going on in this book. You can't sit down and read the Book of Daniel as you would a novel. You have to study it and use the rest of the Bible to interpret its symbols. That's one of the locks that God provides to keep curious minds from getting into this book without an adequate background in Scripture, for without that background you can't understand what's going on.

There's a second precaution that God has taken, and this is the heart of my message. The prophetic section of Daniel doesn't come first in the book. The first six chapters bring us into an understanding of the moral character of God and the character that God requires of the reader. Before you begin to understand the programme, you have to learn how to behave as God wants you to behave. You can't understand the last section unless you have lived through, and understood, what's involved in the first six chapters. You must grasp their moral lessons; you can't cheat, you have to analyse them and experience them in your own life, before you begin to really understand prophecy. You cannot understand the prophetic teaching of the Bible with just your intellect.

Daniel had an incredible view of coming events. But he didn't say, 'Well, the Lord's coming so I don't need to bother being a good civil servant running this nation. I'll just sit and wait for the Lord to come.' Many young people, hearing teaching about the return of Christ, say, 'Well—that means I don't have to work at my exams; the Lord is coming!' I even hear preachers say, 'It's all for the flames anyway—why care about it so much?' There never was a better civil servant in history than Daniel. Don't ever let anybody hear you say that a believer is so heavenly minded he's of no earthly use.

Because he had a perspective of the future—as the first six chapters show us—he was able to be what he was. You can draw all the charts, explain all the symbols, analyse the prophecy of Daniel down to a midge's eyebrow; but if you haven't incorporated the practical teaching of the first part of the book into your own life, you will discover nothing there to enrich your life.

There's no section of Scripture more helpful for living the Christian life in difficult situations. Are you working in a firm surrounded by people taking the name of God in vain? Then this is for you. Are you a teenager at school or college surrounded by those who seem to have no interest in the things of God and his character? Then remember that Daniel and his friends were themselves teenagers in the early chapters of this book. We are shown the pressures they experienced and the values they stood for. Remember, the first stand that Daniel took for the lordship of his God over his life was in the area of education; it had to do with the Jewish food laws, which had symbolic spiritual meaning. He refused to eat the king's meat because it was offered to idols.

It wasn't just that it was a bad dietary law. Some people

won't eat anything unless it is given cover in the Old Testament. You will remember that our friend Peter was shown that what God had made clean he wasn't to call unclean; that meant, they say, that pigs were once unhygienic but bacon is now hygienic because Christ has come into the world. Nonsense! The New Testament teaches very clearly that in the Old Testament there was symbolic meaning. When you have an appetite, whether it be sexual, physical, or aesthetic, you have to hold a careful rein upon it because the Lordship of Christ in our lives, by the power of the Spirit, places constraint on those appetites. That's what the food laws spoke of, among other things. The Jewish people were different, set apart by what they ate; and what they ate had spiritual meaning for them.

We're not tied to those laws now, but the simple fact is that our appetites still have to be kept under constraint. Daniel said, 'I won't eat it.' He didn't jump up and down and said, 'I won't have your rotten meat, it's offered to these gods and I don't like them; it's only the Lord who is Lord...' He didn't have a confrontation, he had a creative alternative. He said, 'I'll have salad instead.' What a godly stand!

And he took a first-class honours degree in the University of Babylon. Chaldean literature wasn't spiritual literature, but he knew and understood it and gained a first-class degree in it. That young person stood for the lordship of his God over his life in the area of education.

In other chapters we read of science. Nebuchadnezzar brought his clever men to try and find out things, but Daniel had the answer, and explained how that God knows that which exists before creation. Science can only deal with what it sees. The laws of tennis do not explain why people play tennis. The scientist will tell you the world is this, that and the other, but he cannot answer the question 'Why is there a world?' Science cannot deal with why.

Nebuchadnezzar announces a massive statue in the valley, 90 feet high, 9 feet thick. He summons all the notables and officers of state in Babylon to its dedication and says, 'Bow down to the statue.' The three men say no. The prophets taught that Jewish people were to submit to the Gentiles and obey the powers that be. That was difficult medicine, but it was the teaching of the word. No revolt in the name of Jehovah was allowed. Yet here is an exception. They refused point blank to obey the civil authorities. They didn't lead a revolt, but they refused to obey the civil power in this area.

The normal behaviour of Christians to civil power is submission. 'What about this tribute?' they said to the Lord Jesus.

'Show me a denarius,' He said, 'whose image is this?'

'Caesar's,' they said.

'Render to Caesar what belongs to Caesar,' said Christ, 'and to God the things that belong to Him.' He chose to answer in the category of ownership. 'That belongs to him, this belongs to God.' And if you're a believer, you are called to worship Him alone. We don't worship the creation, we worship the Creator. If the civil authority says, 'We are God, you must bow down to us', then the Christian just as much as Shadrach, Meshach and Abednego must say 'In that area we worship God alone. We obey God rather than men.' For example, we honour our Queen but will not worship her. In this nation we are very thankful for her. The life she has led and her tact and wisdom over forty years or more in this nation are, so far as I know, unparalleled in my generation. We honour her, we thank God for her, but we don't worship her. Nor would she wish us to.

We have a free and democratic government—but we don't worship it, we worship God alone. Young people, you have many heroes—sports heroes, you name it. You don't worship them. Or—do you? Do you perhaps give them the allegiance that you should be giving to the Lord Jesus? 'Let's kill the heir,' said the vineyard workers, 'so we can have the vineyard for ourselves' (cf. Luke 20). 'No,' says Christ. 'You belong to me.' My dear friends, God ultimately owns this world, and the owner has got some tremendous refurbishing ideas for the future. The Messiah is the owner. We are given the stewardship.

In the garden Peter took his sword and cut off Malchus' ear. Jesus said, 'Put your sword away. If My kingdom were of this world, then would My servants fight.' Do you think Peter was afraid of the Romans? I don't think so. But when Jesus said, 'My kingdom is not of this world and you don't promote

My interests, laws and gospel by violent means,' it seems to me that that is why the disciples forsook Him and fled. They thought, 'If that's what He wants, leave Him to it. We thought He would take Israel from the Romans. We thought He would set up His own kingdom, and we would have fought for it. But if He's going to stand there and let them overwhelm Him and crucify Him on a cross...'. What a lesson they had to learn!

And all across the world you and I are called, if we belong to Him, to stand up for His lordship. 'Worship it,' said Nebuchadnezzar.

'No. We won't worship it.'

Perhaps their families tried to dissuade them from their stance. 'All you have to do is bow down. Do it, but don't believe it.' Wouldn't it have been easy just to say, 'Oh, why bother!' It's rather like a young Israelite, commanded to choose a wife from among those who loved the Lord, falling in love with a Canaanite girl and sitting at the table of the Canaanites. All around him they'd start offering their food to their gods. And he might say, 'Sure! What does it matter? I'm in love. Doesn't matter about God's narrow laws, we're far too narrow in Israel anyway. Why bother? I don't need to honour the lordship of God. I mean, it's love! I love the girl.'

'Do you love her more than Me?' says God.

And it got so bad that there was no difference between the Israelites and the Philistines. That's why when Samson was sent he fulfilled what God sent him to do. The angel said to his mother, 'Your child will make a difference. He will begin to deliver Israel.' And he did. I tell you, when he stuck those torches between the tails of those foxes and burnt those corn stacks, it was a fire, it was better than nothing (cf. Judg. 15). The people said, 'Who did this?'

'Oh, this fellow of strength, Samson.'

'Who carried these gates for thirty miles?'

Imagine if you met him with the gates of the city. 'Hello Samson, good morning, where are you going? Where do you get the strength from?' The Philistines loved strength. They sent out the mighty Goliath. He was strong, look at the physical prowess of the man. And when Goliath went down the valley to fight the Lord with strength—and they sent out this little stripling of a teenager, David, to bring him down— why, the Philistines worshipped strength.

They had a god called Dagon they made with their own hands and his head fell off one day. What do you do with a god whose head falls off? You pick it up with your own strength and put it back on again. But when we face trials and difficulty we don't carry our God, our God carries us. 'Where is Nebo now?' says the sarcastic mighty Isaiah, 'whom you used to carry through the streets of Babylon on your feast days? Where is he now, when these hoards are coming against you? In the back of an ox cart' (Isa. 46).

'What is the secret of Samson?' they kept crying. 'Where does he get his strength?' they asked Delilah. It was strength and he had it. They did not know for a long time, did they, that the secret was the Lord who gave him the strength.

Tell me, what does a stranger feel when they come in here to a Keswick Convention evening like this? What do they feel? Where are we different? Would there *be* a difference? If the Lord's presence is not among us in these evenings, no matter how much I preach, no matter how much we sing, no matter how well we try and do our best, if He doesn't come with us, then carry us not up hence (cf. Exod. 33:15).

'I'll send an angel with you, Moses.'

'No. If you don't come, Lord I'm not going.'

'We're not bowing down to that God. No.'

What does worship mean? Sometimes we think that it's hymns and feelings, a good feeling towards the Lord Jesus. But it's more than that. Worship in the ultimate sense means bowing down to the ultimate authority. What does that mean? Satan says to Christ, 'I'll give you all the kingdoms of the world if you sing some choruses to me in my favour, if you bow down and worship me.' Not 'Hold a few meetings to promote my lordship'; but 'Recognise I am the ultimate principle in this world and in the affairs of men. You have to compromise with me.'

The kingdoms and power of this world can seem very attractive. Young people, a word to you especially. You know, for those of us who are older the world isn't as attractive as it once was, because we've found by experience that it's a cul-de-sac. But you haven't found that out yet. May you learn it tonight; if you want the power and glory of this world, then you have to compromise with Satan. Jesus said, 'Worship the Lord thy God and Him only shalt thou serve.'

'Then it's Calvary for You,' says Satan. 'I'll meet You there.'

These young men were not only worshipping God alone. What were they doing? Take hold of this; they were striking a blow for human freedom. You may say, 'How could three fellows going to a fiery furnace because they wouldn't bow to some silly earthly god be striking a blow for human freedom?' Let me put it this way: for a human being to be asked to bow down before a government of fellow human beings, worship it and give it unquestioning, ultimate, absolute support spells a slavery and an indignity fearful to contemplate.

The world will yet see the harvest of its atheistic, materialistic theories which are currently being taught in our Western world. If there is no God, then something has to be acknowledged as the ultimate power to which we must bow. How do you control men and women? You have to engage their loyalty. And if it's not God, then what? I stood by Lenin's mausoleum in Moscow. The man with me said, 'There's no God; I just believe in my mother and my father and my children.' I replied, 'But look what you have put in His place; the dead body of Lenin; and there's a queue out there a mile long to see him.' Thank God, it's swept away now. But what's going to come in its place across the CIS?

Eventually the Bible teaches that the Antichrist will come. What will he be? He will be man deified. The world will worship man, and if he get's going to have complete power, where will we be? The Bible teaches that the Lord will come and destroy him, and He will rule from shore to shore.

What a fantastic treat there is here! You might say, 'So it's a Jack and the Beanstalk story then—a great miracle comes in.' Well, I don't think it was like that for the three the night before. They said, 'If our God doesn't deliver us, we're going anyway.' Esther was delivered, but these three fellows at this time had to go through the agony of what they had to go endure in the fiery furnace.

Do you have a loved one who was, perhaps, beaten to

death during the war? Some of you have lost your loved ones, they never came home and you're lonely tonight. Do you have a dear one who's died recently of an incurable disease— and you prayed and prayed and it didn't happen, the miracle didn't come? Some, says Hebrews 11, were delivered from the fire. Others were sawn asunder. But whatever happens to us, we say to you tonight, Jesus Christ is Lord. And whatever it costs us we are saying before Him tonight—I trust you are saying with me in your heart—'Lord Jesus, You are Lord alone even if it means that I have to die for it.'

They were tied, thrown in the fire. They gave up the perishable to go for the imperishable. And when for the Lord's sake they let go of all the earthly glory that could have been theirs, when they let go all their own plans, their own ideas for the Lord's sake, the minute they let them go—they were free! 'There are four men loose in there,' Nebuchad-nezzar said. 'Three men loose, and the fourth is like the Son of God.'

Are you holding on to something tonight? 'Jesus is Lord'—but—'I want this or that'...'Jesus is Lord'—but— 'I'm determined to become this or that, whether He likes it or not'...'Jesus is Lord'—but—but—but...

No buts. Say, 'Lord, I surrender all. All this Thou hast done for me. It's a reasonable service, that I no longer have plans of my own.' A crucified man does not have any plans of his own. He can only look in one direction. We are crucified with Christ, aren't we? And because we are crucified with Christ, His plans, not ours apply.

The men are walking free. If you let go of the temporary you'll find the eternal.

The fire did burn something on those young men. It burnt the bonds that bound them, it set them to walk free. So are all God's trials that come towards us designed to do; to free us from things that would shackle us by holding a place in our affection and loyalty that only God Himself should hold. The Lord has sent the fire into your life and circumstances, Chris-tian, to set you free, to wean you away from your own cleverness and dependency on your own plans and ideas and plans for the future. We show what kind of a God He is by our preparedness for sacrifice for Him.

He owns the world, He owns the land. Judas said, 'I want a bit for myself.' Luke in Acts says he bought a field. There's nothing wrong with buying a field—but 'for himself'—is it any wonder it led down to death? That's where that path always leads ultimately. We must say, 'That field I have, O Lord—it's Yours. That home I have, Lord—it's Yours. My family, all my plans—Yours Lord Jesus, You have complete sway.' Not, 'I want a little bit for myself. And if I have to deny Jesus in front of others to get it, well, so what?'

God will see to it, Christian, that you and I will have to make the choice. His lordship, or ours? You are not big enough to be the ultimate goal of your own life. Only He is. There's the challenge. And instead of being bound, the three were set free. May you go out in the freedom of the Lordship of Jesus this night with a joy that is unspeakable and full of glory. Whatever it is that is holding up the blessing, let it go! Anything that comes between me and my Lord's complete place of lordship in my life is wrong. There's the challenge.

The act of the three men led to the worship of that godless king and the transformation of a society. I was talking to somebody today at Keswick and we were saying that we felt great things were afoot. Haven't you felt a lovely spirit in these meetings? That our God is going to do great things in our land again? The great preachers who have stood here down the years have handed their flag on to us. Let's unfurl it! Christian, let it fly from the castle of your heart! And may this Keswick Convention lead to a mighty spiritual awakening in Britain for our day and generation. Maybe it will start tonight.

'SOMETHING BETTER'

by Mr Peter Maiden

John 16:5-15

It must have been marvellous for the Children of Israel. They
had the cloud and the pillar of fire to lead them—visible,
tangible evidence of the living God and of His great care for
them. Yet it must have been even better for the disciples.
Imagine it! Walking with Jesus, conversing with Him, not
reading about His life in a book but seeing first-hand those
miracles happening right in front of their eyes. But throughout John 16, Jesus is preparing His disciples for the day, now
very close, when He is going to leave them. Verse 20: 'You
will weep and lament, you will be sorrowful.' But (He adds),
'Your sorrow will be turned to joy...' Now, how could that
ever be? How could the sorrow of losing Jesus ever be turned
to joy? He says something even more remarkable in verse 7:
'But I tell you the truth, it is to your advantage that I go
away' (New American Standard version). You can imagine
the surprise of the disciples. 'How could it ever be advantageous, not to have Christ in person among us?'

Jesus leaves us in no doubt about the answer. 'If I do not
go away, the Helper [the Holy Spirit] shall not come to you;
but if I go, I will send Him to you.'

The only possible conclusion to be drawn from these statements is that it is more advantageous to have the Holy Spirit
performing His present ministry in the church and in the
world than it would be to have Jesus present physically in this
tent in Keswick this evening. 'My going,' Jesus is saying to

the disciples, 'is for your gain. This present physical closeness to you is a poor thing compared to that which will begin when the Holy Spirit comes. You are about to exchange,' He says, 'the companionship which I can only give you from time to time, for the constant indwelling personal power of My Spirit.'

Perhaps you often say, 'I wish Jesus were here in person! Just to see His face, just to hear His words—there are so many questions I would ask Him! If He were here in person it would be so much easier to bow to His lordship.' But He is saying to us tonight, 'I am giving you something better than My physical presence with you.' And the rest of this chapter shows why the promised ministry of the Holy Spirit would be so vital to the disciples.

Jesus tells them first of the difficult days they are about to face. He warns them (verse 32) that the close companionship and mutual support they've enjoyed for these three wonderful years is about to be violently and abruptly ended. They are going to be scattered, and they will face two main problems. They will be ostracised within their community, and they will face violence. 'They will make you outcasts from the synagogue' (verse 2). You can imagine what that would mean in the deeply religious Jewish society; they would face violence in the name of God. 'They will kill you,' Jesus says, 'and think that thereby they are actually offering service to God.'

Can you imagine the pressures, the isolation that must have entailed for the disciples? The word would have got around, much as the *fatwa* against Salman Rushdie has circulated in sectors of the Moslem community.

The titles of the Holy Spirit

With such incredible difficulties ahead they certainly needed great help. Look now at the two titles that the Lord Jesus gives to the Holy Spirit in this chapter.

The Paraclete
In verse 7 He's called the 'Helper' or 'Counsellor'. The Greek word is *parakletos*. You'll see what *para* means if you

visit the various booths in the street outside this tent where many organisations that try to come alongside the church to help in her witness and her ministry are exhibiting. Such organisations are often called 'parachurch' organisations. 'Paraclete' means exactly that: someone who comes alongside you to help you. There was no way that Jesus could be physically present with these men after they were scattered. So He says, 'Here's something better—a divine Counsellor who will always be there, always be available alongside to help.'

I am reminded of Richard Wurmbrand's testimony, in one of his early books, speaking of his solitary confinement in a Romanian jail. 'Stripped of everything, the presence of Christ was so real to me. His joy was so real that I felt that I would burst if I did not give it expression.' They thought he was in solitary confinement, but the Helper, the Counsellor, the Comforter, the Paraclete was right there alongside to help.

In a few days you will be leaving Keswick and this Convention. I want to say very simply to you: as you and I move away from this Convention, the Holy Spirit is right alongside to help, to empower, to inspire you to be a true disciple of Jesus Christ. In days of difficulty, Jesus says, 'I'm giving you the Helper.'

The Spirit of truth
That title is followed by the promise to guide us into all truth. I love the certainty of those words! He *will* guide you. In times of stress and difficulty such as the disciples were about to face, it's vital to know that you have a truthful guide, a Counsellor you can turn to at any time, always available alongside to help. Emotions rise in stressful times: your mind becomes confused and even your close friends find it difficult to be honest with you, when they see that you're hurting. But the Holy Spirit can never be anything other than His nature. He is the Spirit of truth, and His counsel is always available and totally reliable. He's there alongside to help.

The ministries of the Holy Spirit

Let's look at one of the particular ministries of the Holy

Spirit mentioned in this chapter, which again is so vital in times of difficulty. The last two verses of the previous chapter give the context. Jesus has been explaining how His disciples would be hated by the world. And then He says, 'When the Counsellor comes, whom I will send to you from the Father, the Spirit of truth who goes out from the Father, He will testify about me; but you also must testify' (15:26-27, NIV).

So, Jesus says, there are to be two witnesses, even in a world which hates you: the witness of the Spirit, and your witness. We're not called to retreat in days of difficulty. We're not even called merely to survive. We are called— even in days of difficulty—to be witnesses. But in that also we are never alone, because as we bear witness the Holy Spirit is at work alongside helping. And what particularly is that work? Verses 8-11: as we witness He convicts the world concerning sin, righteousness and judgement.

One of the ways it will be known whether this Convention has been fruitful and effective will be the impact it has on our witness to the world. I've been reading a new book recently by Ron Davies called *I Will Pour Out My Spirit*, a history and theology of revivals. This is what he says.

> The history of the modern protestant missionary movement is to a large extent the history of revivals. As with evangelism, when the church is revived and filled with true divine life there is an irresistible urge to communicate the message of new life to others and a willingness to sacrifice all, out of gratitude for the amazing grace of God experienced by those who consider themselves to be completely unworthy.[1]

Jesus says 'I am giving you my Spirit, and as you receive my Spirit you are to be my witnesses. And my promise is that the Spirit of Truth will bear witness He will bear witness alongside bringing conviction to the human heart.'

The great certainties

Let us look thirdly at the great certainties which the ministry of the Spirit would bring into their lives. Because I want you and me to leave this Convention firmly standing on certainties!

These are difficult days to live the Christian life. Some of you are feeling the cuts and bruises of the battle. Keswick is like an oasis for you. But soon you'll go back to a stressful, difficult situation. Maybe you brought your stresses and difficulties with you and you're struggling with them right now in this meeting. Well, Jesus never promised it would be any different. But He did give some wonderful promises to sustain us in and through those difficulties. I want to mention three promises by pointing out four phrases from the chapter. Verse 23: 'In that day' Jesus says, 'you will no longer ask me anything.' Verse 23: 'My Father will give you whatever you ask in my name.' Verse 27: 'The Father himself loves you'. And finally verse 33: 'I have overcome the world'.

These phrases contain three great certainties for days of difficulty because of the ministry of the Holy Spirit.

The promise of assurance
These disciples were full of questions. Look at verse 17. What does Jesus mean? In that day of the Spirit, He says, certainties will replace doubts and questions.

Think of some of the disciples' questions. Peter asked, 'Lord, where are You going?' Thomas's question was 'How can we know the way?' Philip had a request rather than a question: 'Show us the Father, just let us see the Father.' Doubts, uncertainties. But not after His death, not after His resurrection, not after the gift of the Spirit! Oh, there were still some questions. What about Gentiles being included in the church? How should we deal with the distribution of food to widows? But there was no longer any doubt about the central essential facts of the gospel. The most violent persecutions could not shake their conviction. The age of the Spirit is the age of certainty.

I have a friend who likes to pick up his Bible when he's preaching and say, 'I've read this book from the beginning to the end, including the last chapter. And what do we find when we read the whole book? We win!' I hope you're going to go away from Keswick with that firm conviction ringing in your hearts, 'We are on the victory side.'

Though we've no need to ask Him questions, that same verse 23 assures us that if we make petitions in Christ's name they certainly will be answered. It's a promise that can very easily be misunderstood. It's not a magic formula, guaranteeing you can have whatever you want so long as you add 'in the name of Jesus' to your request. When I was a child I wanted a bike. At that time I was reading these verses. I thought, this is very easy: 'A bike, Lord, in the name of Jesus.' But the bike never arrived.

Chapter 15 of this Gospel shows that praying in Christ's name is absolutely linked with abiding in Christ. The meaning is that if we want true effectiveness and fruitfulness in prayer then it is essential to be abiding in Christ each day; walking with Him, living in obedience. For, Jesus says to His disciples, people who live like that can be assured of a powerful prayer life. The age of the Spirit is an age of assurance.

The promise of the Father's love

Now, what do verses 26 and 27 mean? Jesus is certainly not saying that He'll no longer intercede for us before the Father. His high-priestly ministry is totally essential. Jesus is stressing the access we have to the Father and the acceptance we have before Him in Christ. These are wonderful words: 'The Father himself loves you.' And I hope you're utterly convinced this evening, and that you'll be utterly convinced as you move away from this Convention, of the certainty of your Father's love for you.

The promise of victory

The final verse of the chapter is remarkable. Jesus has been telling the disciples the difficulties that lay ahead for them: but think what lay ahead for Him—the Garden of Gethsemane, the trial, the crucifixion. Yet He says to His disciples, 'Take heart! I have overcome the world.'

The world would look on and see in a man hanging on a cross in utter defeat. But we know tonight that in dying He was overcoming. We know that His death was Satan's defeat. The very worst that Satan could throw at our Saviour, our leader, He made into glorious victory.

Now, let's try to put all this together. Every believer possesses the Holy Spirit. His present ministry brings greater advantages to us than did His physical presence with His disciples during those wonderful three years. Intermittent companionship has been replaced by His constant abiding

presence and power. That's particularly vital when the going
gets rough. He's the Helper, constantly alongside; so they
may ostracise you in society, but never separate you from His
companionship. He is the Spirit of Truth; the counsel He
gives is one hundred percent reliable. Even in the most
difficult days, the most difficult circumstances, I am called to
witness: but in that I'm never alone. The Holy Spirit is
involved alongside, with that constant world-wide ministry of
conviction.

'So particularly in these difficult days,' Jesus says, 'meditate on these three promises which result from My Spirit's
ministry.' The promise of assurance and of answered prayer
as you pray in the Spirit; the promise of our Father's love;
and the promise of sharing in the victory of our Saviour.

Do you see now why Jesus said, 'It's to your advantage
that I go. Because if I don't go you will not receive this
incredible friendship and ministry of the Holy Spirit'? What a
friend to have tonight—the Holy Spirit! Are you enjoying
His friendship? Are you enjoying the fruits of it? Do you
know that constant companionship alongside to help? Many
of us would have to confess that the friendship is not as close
as it should be. And I don't really need to explain the reason
for that, do I? We know that the Holy Spirit can be grieved,
His ministry in our lives can be quenched.

So to close, I want to remind you of three biblical com-
mands. If you and I obey them we will enjoy those three
wonderful certainties and promises that I've mentioned.

Don't grieve the Holy Spirit (Ephesians 4:30)
You see, He's a person. He's not just an influence or a
power—but a sensitive Person hating anything which offends
His holy nature. John Stott writes, 'Since He's the Holy Spirit
He's always grieved by unholiness, and since He's the one
Spirit disunity always causes Him grief.' But not only can He
be grieved by evil, His ministry in and through our lives can
be quenched, subdued or supressed. So what subdues the
ministry of the Spirit in us and through us?

'Don't quench the Holy Spirit' (1 Thessalonians 5:19)
Or, 'Don't put out the Spirit's fire', as the NIV has it. Look at
the verses which surround this exhortation. Look at verse 16,

'Be joyful always; pray continually; give thanks in all circumstances.' These exhortations have to do with our response to God's word. We are to respond to it with worship and thanksgiving. Now look at the exhortations that follow: 'Do not treat prophecies with contempt. Test everything. Hold on to the good. Avoid every kind of evil.' They are about allowing God to speak to us: listening to Him, responding and applying His word to our lives.

The promise of Scripture is that if you and I remain sensitive and obedient in those areas, the fire will continue to burn. But whenever I cease to respond to God's word, and whenever that word of God no longer moves me to thanksgiving and praise, the flames will burn low. It could happen right here, couldn't it, in the middle of this Convention. You've heard so much from God. Am I or are you becoming over-familiar, this week, with holy things? How are you responding? With comparison—or conviction? Do you go away comparing—'Oh, he was good, but not as good as... The Convention this year was as good/wasn't as good as last week/last year...' Is that how you respond?

Or have you come to Keswick to hear God's voice and to respond?

If we have not, you and I are in serious danger of allowing the fire of the Holy Spirit to flame low, to burn low, in our lives.

Be filled with the Spirit (Ephesians 5:18)

Don't grieve Him; don't quench Him; be filled with the Holy Spirit. The New English Bible says, 'Let the Holy Spirit fill you.' So this isn't something which you can learn, it's not a technique you can perform at a particular time. It's something the sovereign Spirit does.

It's interesting that in the parallel passage in Colossians 3:16 Paul writes, 'Let the word of Christ dwell in you richly.' It takes us back to quenching the Spirit. If we respond with obedient worship as God speaks to us, if we let the word of Christ dwell in us richly, then the fire of His Spirit will continue to burn in our lives as we are continually filled with the Holy Spirit.

In Greek this is the present continuous tense—fullness of the Spirit, unlike justification, is not a once-for-all experience we can never lose. It's a privilege in which we have to be continuously renewed by faith and by obedience. That is not to deny or decry particular spiritual crisis-experiences at times in our lives. A friend of mine is fond of saying, 'Any crisis which is not followed by a process will soon become an abscess.' I think there's truth in that. Let's have those crisis-experiences—I've had them from time to time in my life—but let that daily, weekly annual process go on, letting the Holy Spirit fill us.

I used to think of the fullness of the Spirit as rather like filling a bottle; there came a point when it was full. And unless some was used or spilled, you couldn't put more in. Then I was encouraged to think in terms of a river: the constant flowing of the Spirit through our lives, and therefore the constant need of His filling. Do you remember the words of Jesus on the last day of the feast in John 7?

> Jesus stood up and said in a loud voice, 'If any man is thirsty, let him come to me and drink. Whoever believes in me, as the Scripture has said, streams of living water will flow from within him.' By this he meant the Spirit, whom those who believed in him were later to receive.

What a lovely picture! Thirsty, hungry Christians, drinking from the fountain of the Lord Jesus Christ and allowing those streams of the Spirit, streams of living water, to flow through them as they are constantly filled by the Spirit of God. Brothers and sisters, are we going to be thirsty for a week of Convention? Or are we going to be thirsty for a lifetime? And in that daily thirsting for God, will we allow the Holy Spirit to constantly fill us, flooding out from us, touching barren lives, touching arid situations and transforming them so that God is glorified by His Spirit's ministry through our lives? May God bless His word to us.

Note

1. Ron Davies, *I will Pour Out My Spirit* (Monarch, 1992).

KESWICK 1992 TAPES AND VIDEOS

Tapes

Here is a list of tape numbers for each of the addresses included in this volume, in the order in which they appear:

Mr Derick Bingham	31, 32, 33, 34
Dr Raymond Brown	1, 2, 3, 4
Mr Chua Wee Hian	6
Rev. Tom Houston	7
Dr Raymond Brown	16
Canon Keith Weston	8
Mr Jonathan Lamb	10
Rev. Philip Hacking	37
Rev George Hoffman OBE	38
Mr Derick Bingham	39
Mr Peter Maiden	40

Tapes cost £2.95 plus postage (1 tape 45p, 2 tapes 60p, 3 tapes 70p, 4 tapes 80p, 5-6 tapes £1). Orders should be sent to:

ICC (International Christian Communications)
Silverdale Road
Eastbourne
East Sussex BN20 7AB

A full catalogue including many previous Keswick addresses is available from the same address.

Video

Video recordings are available as follows:

Mr Derick Bingham	KES92 2/22, 2/24, 2/28, 2/30
Dr Raymond Brown	KES92 1/05, 1/08, 1/14, 1/17
Mr Chua Wee Hian	No video
Rev. Tom Houston	KES92 1/107
Dr Raymond Brown	No video
Canon Keith Weston	KES92 1/10
Mr Jonathan Lamb	KES92 1/16
Rev. Philip Hacking	KES92 2/23
Rev George Hoffman OBE	KES92 2/25
Mr Derick Bingham	KES92 2/27
Mr Peter Maiden	KES92 2/29

Videos cost £9.99 plus £1 postage per video. Tapes, and a full catalogue including many other Keswick addresses, are availble from:

Mr D. Armstrong
STV Videos
Box 299, Bromley, Kent BR2 9XB.

KESWICK 1993

The annual Keswick Convention takes place each July at the heart of England's beautiful Lake District. The two separate weeks of the Convention offer an unparalleled opportunity for listening to gifted Bible exposition, experiencing Christian fellowship with believers from all over the world, and enjoying something of the unspoilt grandeur of God's creation.

Each of the two weeks has a series of four morning Bible Readings, followed by other addresses throughout the rest of the day. The programme in the second week is a little less intensive, and it is often referred to as 'Holiday Week'. There are also regular meetings throughout the fortnight for young people, and in the second week for children.

The dates for the 1993 Keswick Convention are 17-24 July (Convention Week) and 24-31 July (Holiday Convention Week). The Bible Reading speakers are Rev. Dr Donald English and Rev. Alistair Begg. Other speakers during the fortnight are Mr Nigel Lee, Rev. Bob Key, Mr Charles Price, Rev. Mark Ashton, Mr Dick Dowsett, Rev. David Coffey and Rev. Ian Coffey.